# Promoting
# Academic
# Achievement
# Among
# **ENGLISH**
# **LEARNERS**

*To our parents:*
*Loty and Julio Goldenberg, who provided*
*me with a world-class bilingual education (CG)*
*and*
*Cyrella and Leonard Hertzberg, whose lives were*
*examples of commitment, perseverance, and generosity (RC).*

# Promoting Academic Achievement Among ENGLISH LEARNERS

## A GUIDE TO THE RESEARCH

### Claude Goldenberg
### Rhoda Coleman

**CORWIN**
A SAGE Company

*For information:*

Corwin
A SAGE Company
2455 Teller Road
Thousand Oaks, California 91320
(800) 233-9936
Fax: (800) 417-2466
www.corwin.com

SAGE India Pvt. Ltd.
B 1/I 1 Mohan Cooperative
  Industrial Area
Mathura Road, New Delhi 110 044
India

SAGE Ltd.
1 Oliver's Yard
55 City Road
London EC1Y 1SP
United Kingdom

SAGE Asia-Pacific Pte. Ltd.
33 Pekin Street #02-01
Far East Square
Singapore 048763

Printed in the United States of America

*Library of Congress Cataloging-in-Publication Data*

Goldenberg, Claude Nestor, 1954-
Promoting academic achievement among English learners: a guide to the research/Claude Goldenberg and Rhoda Coleman.
        p. cm.
Includes bibliographical references and index.
ISBN 978-1-4129-5549-2 (pbk.)
    1. Academic achievement—United States. 2. English language—Study and teaching—United States—Foreign speakers. 3. Bilingual education—United States. I. Coleman, Rhoda II. Title.

LB1062.6.G63 2010
428.2'4—dc22                                    2009048071

This book is printed on acid-free paper.

10   11   12   13   14   10   9   8   7   6   5   4   3   2   1

| | |
|---|---|
| *Acquisitions Editor:* | Dan Alpert |
| *Associate Editor* | Megan Bedell |
| *Editorial Assistant:* | Sarah Bartlett |
| *Production Editor:* | Jane Haenel |
| *Copy Editor:* | Mark Bast |
| *Typesetter:* | C&M Digitals (P) Ltd. |
| *Proofreader:* | Sarah Duffy |
| *Indexer:* | Terri Corry |
| *Cover and Graphic Designer:* | Michael Dubowe |

# Contents

# List of Tables and Figures

## TABLES

## FIGURES

# *Acknowledgments*

S incere thanks to

- our colleagues on the National Literacy Panel and the CREDE synthesis teams, without whose painstaking work this book would not have been possible;
- our editor at Corwin, Dan Alpert, for his outstanding help, support, encouragement, forbearance, and infinite patience;
- Ronald Gallimore, for his helpful feedback and suggestions on the manuscript;
- our spouses, Ellen Goldenberg and Gary Coleman, for putting up with the many intrusions on family life, including frequent late-night phone calls—loving thanks for their support, encouragement, and patience;
- the many educators with whom we have worked and from whom we have learned so much; and
- the external reviewers of the book manuscript, whose questions and suggestions greatly improved the final product:

Alberto Esquinca, Assistant Professor of Bilingual Education and ESL, University of Texas, El Paso, TX

Sandra Mercuri, Assistant Professor of Curriculum and Instruction, The University of Texas at Brownsville and Texas Southmost College, Brownsville, TX

Diep Nguyen, Assistant Superintendent for Instruction, School District 62, Des Plaines, IL

Deborah Palmer, Assistant Professor of Bilingual/Bicultural Education, Department of Curriculum and Instruction, University of Texas, Austin, TX

Needless to say, all errors of fact and interpretation are strictly our own.

# *About the Authors*

**Claude Goldenberg,** a native of Argentina, is professor of education at Stanford University. He received his AB from Princeton University and PhD from UCLA's Graduate School of Education. Goldenberg has taught junior high school in San Antonio, Texas, and first grade in a bilingual elementary school in the Lennox School District near Los Angeles. Goldenberg was a National Academy of Education Spencer Fellow and a recipient (with Ronald Gallimore) of the Albert J. Harris Award from the International Reading Association. He was on the Committee for the Prevention of Early Reading Difficulties in Young Children (National Research Council) and the National Literacy Panel (NIH and U.S. Department of Education), which synthesized research on literacy development among language-minority children and youth. He is the author of *Successful School Change: Creating Settings to Improve Teaching and Learning* (Teachers College, 2004). His research focuses on improving achievement for language-minority students, particularly those from Latino backgrounds.

**Rhoda Coleman** is senior research fellow and professional development specialist at the Center for Language Minority Education and Research at California State University, Long Beach (CSULB). She received her BA and EdD from the University of Southern California, has a master's in reading and a reading specialist credential from Loyola Marymount University, and holds a master's in administration from California State University, Los Angeles. Coleman taught elementary school in Grades 1 through 6 for 29 years in the Lennox School District near Los Angeles, where she taught English learners transitioning into English. She was then a language arts consultant for the Los Angeles County Office of Education, providing K–12 professional development to school districts throughout California and writing and producing over 25 teacher training videos. She currently teaches in the teacher credential program at CSULB. Coleman was a California Teacher of the Year, recipient of the Milken National Educator Award, and California Social Studies Teacher of the Year.

# 1

## *Why This Book?*

The growing number of English language learners (ELLs) in our schools poses increasing challenges and opportunities to U.S. educators and policy makers. A generation or two ago, the achievement of children who came to school knowing little or no English was hardly a national issue. Today, it is. Between 1979 and 2007, the number of school-age children (5- to 17-year-olds) who spoke a language other than English at home nearly tripled,

- Why is it important for educators to have a solid understanding of what research says about improving the achievement of English language learners?
- What kind of research on ELLs is discussed in this book?
- What two reports, published in 2006, provide the most comprehensive look at this research to date?
- What is *this* book's goal?
- Which question or issue has historically dominated research and debate about the education of ELLs?
- What other questions and issues are also important for educators to understand?

from less than 4 million to almost 11 million; children who speak a language other than English now constitute over 20 percent of all children ages 5 to 17 (Planty et al., 2009).

Not all of these students are limited in their English proficiency, of course. But many are, and the ELL population in U.S. schools is growing fast. In 1990, one of every 20 public school students (5 percent) in grades K–12 was limited in English proficiency. Today there are over 5 million ELLs—one in nine, or more than 10 percent of the school-age population. The number of ELLs has grown more than 150 percent since 1990, a period when the overall school population increased by much less (Goldenberg, 2008). Figure 1.1 shows the rate of increase of ELLs between 1989–1990 and

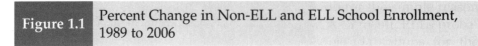

| Figure 1.1 | Percent Change in Non-ELL and ELL School Enrollment, 1989 to 2006 |

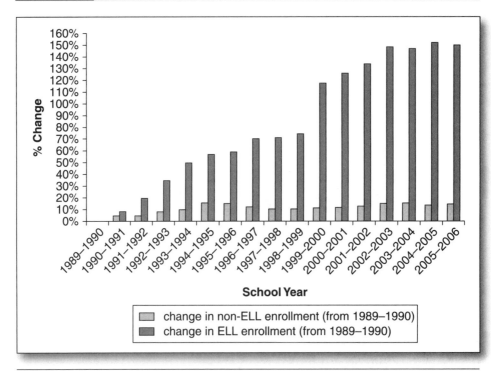

*Source:* The National Clearinghouse for English Language Acquisition and Language Instruction Educational Programs, U.S. Department of Education.

2005–2006 in comparison to the much lower rate of increase in the general school-age population.

Moreover, states not typically associated with English learners—South Carolina, North Carolina, Tennessee, Arkansas, and Indiana—saw an increase in the ELL population from nearly 300 percent to nearly 700 percent in the decade between 1995–1996 and 2005–2006 (http://www.ncela.gwu.edu/faqs). No part of the country remains unaffected by the large increase in ELLs. Even Appalachia has experienced an influx of students from a wide variety of language backgrounds—among them, Spanish, Serbian, Vietnamese, Japanese, and Arabic (Marcus, Adger, & Arteagoitia, 2007). Readers might further be surprised to find out that most ELLs were born in the United States. Seventy-six percent of elementary-age ELLs were born in the United States, as were 56 percent of ELLs in middle through high school. In fact, the parents of about one-fifth of ELLs were also born in the United States (Capps, Fix, Murray, Passel, & Herwantoro, 2005).

Regardless of where they live and where they were born, far too many ELLs never fully master English and fare more poorly compared to children who are English speakers (Goldenberg, 2008). Even those who have been in the United States for several years consistently underperform compared to their native-English-speaking peers. This discrepancy bodes ill for ELLs' future schooling and their vocational options. It also bodes ill for society as a whole, since the costs of large-scale underachievement among large sectors of the populace are very high (Natriello, McDill, & Pallas, 1990).

## A NEW FOCUS ON ENGLISH LEARNERS

The number of English learners was much smaller 30 and 40 years ago, but there was also a different educational ethos: Children out of the English-speaking mainstream were at best second-class citizens. At worst they were invisible, left to "sink or swim" on their own. Thomas Carter (Carter, 1970; Carter & Segura, 1979) and James Crawford (Crawford, 2004), among others, have provided excellent histories of how Spanish-speaking and other language-minority (students who come from homes where a language other than English is spoken) children fared in U.S. schools and why parents, community members, activists, and educators began to demand equitable treatment. Today, thanks to court cases, legislation, national and state accountability mandates, growing numbers, *and* increased acceptance that all children deserve a fair chance at educational success, many educators and policy makers are at least attempting to meet the challenge more productively, even if with considerable uncertainty—and not without controversy.

Passage of the No Child Left Behind (NCLB) Act in 2001, the foundational federal legislation governing federal policy in elementary and secondary education in the first decade of this century, raised the stakes for educators higher than ever. There has been increased pressure for all children to achieve at levels that will provide them with access to the educational, social, and economic mainstream. As part of NCLB's school accountability measures, schools cannot meet their Adequate Yearly Progress (AYP) goals unless all major subgroups at the school—including ELLs—meet achievement targets. Teachers of ELLs, as well as site and district administrators, are under tremendous pressure. Many argue that the pressure is unfair, is misguided, and has done more harm than good. Moreover, as of this writing, it is unclear in what form, if any, NCLB will be reauthorized and what the accountability requirements will be. Regardless, it is imperative that teachers, administrators, and policy makers understand the state of our knowledge regarding how to improve the achievement of students who arrive at our schools less than fully proficient in English. This is true with or without the high-stakes accountability of NCLB or any other legislation.

To help in the effort to improve outcomes for ELLs, two major government-funded reviews of the research were published in 2006: *Developing*

*Literacy in Second-Language Learners: Report of the National Literacy Panel on Language-Minority Children and Youth* (August & Shanahan, 2006) and *Educating English Language Learners* (Genesee, Lindholm-Leary, Saunders, & Christian, 2006), prepared by researchers associated with the Center for Research on Education, Diversity, and Excellence (CREDE). These reports have synthesized a complex and difficult research base to try to provide educators, policy makers, and maybe even researchers with a clear view of the current state of knowledge on promoting academic success among ELLs. The reports, like many aspects of the research base itself, are complex, technical, and filled with theoretical and conceptual issues that are challenging to sort through. We decided to base this book largely on these two reports (supplemented, as we will point out, with other sources) because they are the most comprehensive and ambitious reviews of the research pertaining to the education of ELLs that exist.[1]

We wish to be clear that we use the term *research* in a very specific way. As most people know, there are many different types of educational research. There are quantitative and qualitative, experimental and correlational, ethnographic and observational, survey and interview, and many other types. The research we focus on here is that which includes at least some data on some type of student educational outcome. We define *outcome* very broadly, since there are many possible educational outcomes. There are tests, certainly, both standardized and nonstandardized. But there are outcomes in terms of student behavior, engagement, motivation, writing, and speaking, to name just a few. Any student behavior or by-product that can reasonably be construed to be the result of, or influenced by, some educational process (e.g., a teaching strategy) or educational context (e.g., a particular classroom environment) can be construed as an outcome.

We have heard, read, and even been in too many unproductive discussions where someone immediately equates outcomes with standardized test scores. The two are not synonymous. Standardized test scores are a *type* of outcome that provides a certain *type* of information about students. But, obviously, standardized tests are limited. *Any* single way of trying to gauge what students know and can do (or want to do and will do) is limited. This is why we take a very broad view of what constitutes an outcome. Those who actually read what we say about the studies we discuss—rather than assume we only consider experiments evaluated with standardized tests—will realize that we draw on a wide range of studies that define and gauge outcomes in various ways. Reducing the belief that we need to look at outcomes to an argument for or against standardized test scores misses the point. In fact, it does a great disservice to furthering our understanding in this and other critical educational areas.

---

[1]We would note that the National Literacy Panel report has had its critics (Cummins, 2009; Pray & Jiménez, 2009).

In this book we consider studies that try to determine the effect of an educational process or context on some sort of student outcome. To do this, a study actually had to *collect* data on one or more student outcomes. It might surprise readers to know that many studies do not collect data, much less report findings, relative to student outcomes—at least not directly. They might describe and analyze a classroom or classroom practices and make some judgment about whether it is a desirable place for students. Or they might compare school and home environments and analyze what about the school might help or hinder the learning of different students. For the most part we do not draw on studies such as these because they cannot tell us very much about the relationship between educational processes or contexts on the one hand and student outcomes on the other. They can provide insights into complex educational processes, but they do not directly link these processes to educational outcomes for students.

We draw on a range of study types. No study was excluded from consideration because it was qualitative; although most of the studies discussed here are quantitative, and quite a few had some sort of experimental design, we also draw on qualitative studies, as long as they met the criterion that data were collected and reported on some sort of student outcome. There was no requirement that only experiments or standardized tests be used. The requirement was that the researcher, in some way, collect data on student outcomes—broadly defined—and relate them to some educational process, usually at school.

## THIS BOOK'S GOAL

The goal of this book is to make transparent for educators, policy makers, and any interested reader what these reports and some of the research that has appeared since their publication say about promoting academic success among ELLs. The need for such a book became manifestly clear when one of us (Coleman) conducted a study on how school districts decided on programs for ELLs. To an alarming degree (although not unique in education), decisions were driven by theoretical orientation or personal preference and philosophy. Some district-level decision makers, such as the one quoted below, understood the gaps in the research (all quotes taken from Coleman, 2006):

> There are only theories about what works. Until the research gives us some definitive answers, we're just guessing. There's good things out there, but we need the best. . . . Data will make the difference. It will tell us if *Avenues* [an English language development program] is making a difference.

Others expressed frustration over lack of a coherent, focused, consistent approach to educating English learners:

> I went to the accountability institute from the Department of Education, and they don't have the plan. We need a plan! There's no plan, no prototype, a lot of problems discussed and a lot of expectations, and it's been that way for 20 years. There are a lot of problems. They tell us to do it, but they don't tell us how. They don't know how, and they have nothing to give us. We need to find out what works and have some consistency. A well-trained teacher, a good program, and consistency.

Still others did not see research as much of an issue, program choices being a matter of philosophy:

> We believed in the philosophy of teaching English through content. It had a good reputation. I had heard a lot of schools were using the program. You hear about *Into English* [another English language development program] all the time. Not about data or research. It was more about using it. The beginning pages talk about research, but it didn't really affect the decision. . . . It could be better, but it's good enough, in terms of what's available. It does what we need.

Or, consider the following comment:

> I'm sure the research was included. Its reputation [influenced us], not outcome data. I don't know, we agreed with the philosophy because it fits in with the SDAIE [specially designed academic instruction in English] strategies and BICS [basic interpersonal communicative skills] and CALP [cognitive academic language proficiency]. . . . In my master's class we thoroughly reviewed ELD programs, and *Into English* came out on top. Everyone agreed.

Educators must have a better basis than they do now for making decisions about programs and policies for English learners. This book attempts to help provide such a basis. Knowing the research base includes understanding what the research supports but also what the research does *not* support, either because a particular practice has been discredited or because there is no credible research to help resolve an issue. Understanding the current state of knowledge also includes understanding key controversies and uncertainties. We do not dwell on the controversies and uncertainties, but they are unavoidable, particularly in a field that has historically been politically volatile and theoretically complex, even murky.

We will offer practical suggestions based either on the research or on "best guesses" in the absence of clear research. Each chapter also contains a small scenario to illustrate how some of the recommendations would look in practice in an actual classroom or school. Chapter 8 has scenarios that integrate recommendations relevant to each of the previous chapters. The scenarios in all the chapters are taken from actual teachers' lessons and schoolwide models that were observed during school site visits while conducting research over the past four years. In some cases, particularly in Chapter 8, there are composite illustrations drawn from the best practices of several teachers or schools to show the integration of several elements such as instructional strategies, cultural awareness, and schoolwide implementation practices.

However, this book is neither a manual nor a compendium of teaching strategies. Our hope, rather, is that it will help educators and policy makers adopt or develop policies and programs that promote much higher levels of success for English learners.

Nearly all of this book's content will draw from the two reports mentioned earlier. Researchers on the panels spent two to three years locating, reading, evaluating, and synthesizing research from the preceding 20 to 25 years. The work of these panels provides the essential core for what we write here. The two reports overlap substantially; most important, they reviewed research published from about 1980 to about 2003 on ELLs. The goal of each report was to try to determine what we know from research about improving educational outcomes for these students, that is, what we can do to help them succeed in school. The reports differ in important respects. For example, the National Literacy Panel (NLP) focused exclusively on literacy, whereas the CREDE report looked at a broader range of outcomes; the NLP considered literacy in L1 (the child's native language) and L2 (the societal language the child was acquiring), which, depending on where a study was conducted, was not necessarily English. The CREDE report only looked at outcomes when L2 was English. There were also some methodological differences in how the reviews were conducted and what studies were deemed adequate for inclusion. Some of these issues are noted below and throughout the book when relevant to the issue being addressed. Table 1.1 provides a more detailed comparison of key aspects of the two reports.

This is an evolving field. There have been some new developments since the publication of the studies that informed these reports, although nothing that we are aware of that would significantly change our recommendations. To the extent we can, we draw from published sources and ongoing research to try and round out the picture or fill in gaps. We cite relevant studies that appeared after the NLP and CREDE review period (approximately 1980 to about 2003). For example, early reading intervention studies in both English and Spanish have shown the effectiveness of intensive and focused small-group instruction to help children who are at risk for reading difficulties (see Chapter 3); an oral English language intervention has shown promise as a way of accelerating English language development, whether children are in an English immersion or a bilingual program (see Chapter 4).

**Table 1.1** Comparison of National Literacy Panel (NLP) and Center for Research on Education, Diversity and Excellence (CREDE) Reports

|  | *NLP* | *CREDE* |
|---|---|---|
| **Outcomes of interest** | Literacy | Oral language, literacy, academic achievement |
| **Language of outcome measures** | L2 (usually English) for some chapters; L1 and L2 for others | English only |
| **Included studies of foreign language acquisition?** | Generally no; yes in some chapters but only English as a foreign language | No |
| **Country where studies were conducted** | Worldwide | United States only |
| **Language in which studies were published** | English | English |
| **Consistency of search criteria across chapters** | Varied by chapter | Consistent |
| **Ages** | 3–18 years old | PreK–12th grade |
| **Dates of study publication** | 1980–approximately 2002 | "The last 20 years" |
| **Type of publications** | Peer-reviewed journal articles; some chapters included tech reports and dissertations; no books included | Peer-reviewed journal articles and selected technical reports |
| **Study sample criteria for study's inclusion** | Language-minority students either had to comprise 50 percent of sample or outcome data had to be disaggregated for these students. | Not specified |
| **Methodological criteria for study's inclusion** | For experiments or quasi-experiments, control or comparison group and use of either random assignment or matching criteria to establish comparability. Each group sample included more than four subjects. Programs cited in Chapter 14 | Research design appropriate to the question, research well carried out and described, conclusions supported by the evidence; almost all studies quantitative |

|  | NLP | CREDE |
|---|---|---|
|  | ("Language of Instruction") had at least a six-month span between the onset of instruction and post-tests. For correlational studies, samples had to consist of 20 subjects or more. No comparable inclusion criteria for qualitative studies, which were prominent in three chapters. In Chapter 11 ("Sociocultural Influences"), studies had to report data on some student outcome. |  |
| **Number and specification of search procedures** | Seven searches plus at least five supplementary searches of ERIC, PsycInfo, LLBA, Sociological Abstracts, MEDLINE, MLA; refereed articles from major reviews (e.g., August & Hakuta); table of contents of frequently cited journals; NCELA Web site | ERIC, PsycInfo, LLBA searches; hand searches of select education journals; searches of bibliographies of reviewed articles |

Essentially, then, this book is a synthesis and summary of the two reports (with some key updates), written in a way to address the questions and issues practitioners and policy makers frequently pose. We offer practical recommendations at the end of each chapter and in the book's concluding chapter, supported by the research (or at least our interpretation of it). But where there is no research base to answer a particular question or resolve an issue, we say so. We also try to distinguish between recommendations that are empirically grounded—that is, based on specific studies—and recommendations based on our opinions or best guesses, although sometimes the distinction is difficult to maintain and direct application of findings to recommendations less than straightforward.

Many potentially important new developments have come onto the scene in the past few years. For example, we've seen promising programs and approaches for English language development (Dutro, 2003) and English language instruction to support content area instruction (Schleppegrell, Greer, & Taylor, 2008). No evaluations have been published yet, however. Another example is in the area of assessment. The California English Language Development Test (CELDT), first administered in 2001 and under continual development since, might prove to be a significant advance in assessing English language proficiency. Unpublished technical reports (CTB McGraw-Hill, 2005), however, indicate problems with the cut scores used to determine level of language proficiency (e.g., early intermediate, intermediate) and even whether a student is to be classified ELL or English proficient (Stokes-Guinan & Goldenberg, in press). Unfortunately, assessing English language proficiency, particularly in a way that is instructionally useful for teachers, poses significant challenges with which educators and researchers around the country continue to grapple (Abedi, 2007, 2008).

## WHAT ABOUT BILINGUAL EDUCATION?

The field of language-minority education and research has traditionally been dominated by the bilingual education issue. For years, the key question—sometimes it seemed the *only* question—was: What should be the language (or languages) of instruction for children who come to school less than fully proficient in English? Should they be instructed in their home language (for some period of time or even throughout their school careers)? Or should they be put into English instruction the moment they walk into school? Or somewhere in between?

This already complex issue is further complicated by the question of what our goal is for these students. If the goal is promoting achievement only in English, then the question becomes how much (if any) primary-language instruction is best for maximum achievement in English. However, if the goal is primary-language development and literacy *in addition to* English academic competence—that is, bilingualism and biliteracy—then the answer is likely to be different. Many would argue—and we would agree—that bilingualism ought to be our educational goal (see, most recently, Gándara & Rumberger, 2006), but clearly there is considerable disagreement over this.

The bilingual education question has been extremely controversial and the subject of court cases, state legislation, ballot-box initiatives, op-ed pieces, political statements, and a great deal of posturing and overheated rhetoric. It is a topic about which passions run high, largely because language is not just a technical issue of what instructional method works better. Language is about identity, culture, and history. For many language-minority persons in the United States (and elsewhere around the globe), maintenance of the native language is a way to affirm identity, culture, and history while counteracting discrimination, disempowerment, and disrespect. On the other hand, many U.S. English speakers (and some immigrants who subscribe to what is sometimes not very flatteringly called an "assimilationist" view) stake out a position that is the mirror image: Use—and learn—English. Leave the home language and culture at home to enter the mainstream and become "fully American" (see, for example, Rodriguez, 1982, for a well-known example that stirred a great deal of controversy nearly 30 years ago).

Leaving aside for the moment that using English in school exclusively might not be the way to maximize learning English and academic content *in*

*English* (we leave this to Chapter 2), it is understandable how these two contrasting outlooks have dominated discussions and research about ELL children's schooling. However, the overwhelming focus on language of classroom instruction has served to obscure many other issues and important questions about the education of English learners. This is unfortunate because, as important as language of instruction is, there are many other issues that are probably at least as important. These include quality of instruction (in either the home language or English); promoting oral English proficiency; assessment; and school, district, home, and family factors that influence achievement. The two reports we draw from reviewed a wide range of studies and considered a large number of important questions aside from those having to do with language of instruction. We will do the same.

## ELLs IN THE UNITED STATES: POPULATIONS AND PROGRAMS

The need for valid and reliable information about how to promote ELLs' academic success grows in direct proportion to the number of ELL students in our schools. It might be useful for the reader to have a general sense of the national picture.

According to a survey conducted by the U.S. Department of Education in 2000–2001 (there has been no comparable survey since), students who are limited in their English proficiency come from more than 400 different language backgrounds (Kindler, 2002). Nearly 80 percent were Spanish speakers, but as shown in Table 1.2, hundreds of thousands of English learners speak many other languages. Although the percentages seem tiny in comparison to Spanish, .5 percent of the over 5 million school-age English learners, for example, is more than 25,000 students.

Because the ELL population is not evenly distributed across the country, different states and regions have greater or lesser concentrations of ELLs than others, so the national figures obscure the fact that certain language groups tend to be concentrated in different parts of the country. For example, while speakers of Russian make up less than 1 percent of the U.S. ELL population, there are counties in southern Washington and northern Oregon where the concentration is far greater. Same for the Khmer-speaking population: Nationally these students make up a very small percentage of the ELL population, but in some schools in Long Beach, California, Khmer speakers are 8–10 percent of the ELL population. Individual schools can thus feel an impact from different language groups that national figures do not reveal. (See http://www.mla.org/census_main for a Modern Language Association interactive map showing the locations and number of speakers of 33 languages and language groups in each U.S. state, Washington, D.C., and Puerto Rico.)

| Table 1.2 | Most Frequent 15 Languages Spoken by ELLs | |

| | Home Language | Estimated Percentage of ELLs Who Speak This Language | Approximate Number of ELLs Who Speak This Language* |
|---|---|---|---|
| 1 | Spanish | 79.05 | 4,031,300 |
| 2 | Vietnamese | 1.95 | 99,600 |
| 3 | Hmong | 1.55 | 79,281 |
| 4 | Chinese, Cantonese | 1.02 | 52,055 |
| 5 | Korean | 0.97 | 49,258 |
| 6 | Haitian Creole | 0.93 | 47,316 |
| 7 | Arabic | 0.91 | 46,244 |
| 8 | Russian | 0.82 | 41,627 |
| 9 | Tagalog | 0.75 | 38,239 |
| 10 | Navajo | 0.59 | 30,280 |
| 11 | Khmer | 0.59 | 30,041 |
| 12 | Chinese, Mandarin | 0.49 | 25,065 |
| 13 | Portuguese | 0.46 | 23,287 |
| 14 | Urdu | 0.41 | 20,892 |
| 15 | Serbo-Croatian | 0.38 | 19,227 |

*Based on an estimated 5.1 million school-age ELLs (NCELA, 2008) and assuming percentages have remained the same since the survey year.

Source: Languages and percentages from Kindler's (2002) Survey of the States' Limited English Proficient Students.

The language-minority population in the United States is highly diverse, and we should obviously avoid stereotyping individuals. However, it is a fact that language minorities tend to come from lower socioeconomic backgrounds than the English-speaking U.S. population (www.census.gov/population/www). Whereas nearly 85 percent of adults who speak only English have at least high school degrees, fewer than 50 percent of adults who speak a language other than English and speak English with some difficulty have high school degrees. A similar contrast exists for adults with at least college degrees: Nearly 25 percent of English-only speakers have college or gradu-ate degrees, but only 13 percent of individuals who speak another language and speak English with difficulty have college or graduate degrees. These numbers tell us nothing about why education levels are lower among language-minority adults (see "Correlation and Causation" section later in this chapter), only that they are. And this has implications for educators, since a relatively low level of parental education puts children at risk for rel-atively poor educational outcomes, independent of language spoken and English proficiency (Sirin, 2005).

Differences in the socioeconomic characteristics among the many language-minority populations in the United States are also important to recognize, although, again, we must avoid stereotyping—attributing an average or perceived characteristic to every member of a group. As we have seen, the huge preponderance of ELLs in the United States—80 percent—are of Hispanic or Latino origin. The second-largest group of ELLs (a little under 10 percent) is Asians, a far more diverse group since it includes people whose origins are in a continent with languages and cultures about as diverse as can be imagined. As Table 1.3 illustrates, the socioeconomic characteristics of Latinos and Asians are quite different. Moreover, there are differences *within* these groups such that, for example, Cambodians have a very different demographic profile than Koreans and Mexicans quite dif-ferent from Cubans. From a statistical standpoint, students from groups with lower levels of education and family income will be at greater risk of poor school outcomes, regardless of the language they speak or how well they speak English. The point is that for many ELL students, the challenges they face go beyond becoming fully proficient in English.

Further complicating the picture is that ELLs are in many different types of programs that use students' home languages to a different degree, from not at all to very extensively. Four of the most commonly used program models for ELLs are the following:

- English immersion: All instruction is in English or substantially in English; there is no instruction in primary language (e.g., Spanish) language arts or any other academic area. Usually students have an ELD (English language development) class or period (formerly known as ESL, or English as a second language) specifically geared to developing English language skills.
- Transitional bilingual education: Instruction in language arts and other academic areas is provided in the home language (e.g., Spanish) for the first year to approximately three to four years of a child's schooling, then transitioning to instruction in English only. Programs often include an ELD class or period.
- Maintenance (or developmental) bilingual education (sometimes also called "late exit"): Instruction in language arts and other aca-demic areas is provided in the home language throughout elementary

| Table 1.3 | Education and Income Characteristics of Select Hispanic and Asian Populations | | | | |

| | Total Population | Percentage of High School Graduates | Percentage With a BA or More | Per Capita Income* | Percentage Below Poverty |
|---|---|---|---|---|---|
| **White non-Hispanic** | **194,552,774** | **85.5** | **27.0** | **24,819** | **7.9** |
| **Hispanic/ Latino** | **35,305,818** | **52.4** | **10.4** | **12,111** | **22.1** |
| Mexican | 20,640,711 | 45.8 | 7.5 | 10,918 | 23.3 |
| Puerto Rican | 3,406,178 | 63.3 | 12.5 | 13,518 | 25.1 |
| Cuban | 1,241,685 | 62.9 | 21.2 | 20,451 | 14.3 |
| Salvadoran | 655,165 | 36.1 | 5.5 | 12,349 | 21.2 |
| **Asian** | **10,242,998** | **80.4** | **44.1** | **21,823** | **12.3** |
| Chinese mainland | 2,314,537 | 76.2 | 47.1 | 23,642 | 13.1 |
| Filipino | 1,850,314 | 87.3 | 43.8 | 21,267 | 6.2 |
| Vietnamese | 1,122,528 | 61.9 | 19.4 | 15,655 | 15.7 |
| Korean | 1,076,872 | 86.3 | 43.8 | 18,805 | 14.4 |
| Cambodian | 171,937 | 46.7 | 9.2 | 10,366 | 29.8 |
| Hmong | 169,428 | 40.4 | 7.5 | 6,600 | 37.6 |

*1999 dollars

Source: U.S. Census Bureau American FactFinder *Fact Sheet for a Race, Ethnic, or Ancestry Group* (from 2000 Census).

school, even once children have transitioned into English instruction for much of their school day. Programs often include an ELD class or period.

- Dual language bilingual education: 50–90 percent of instruction for ELLs and for English speakers in the same classroom is provided in the ELLs' home language; English instruction is gradually introduced so that by the end of elementary school the balance is 50–50. Programs can include an ELD class or period.

There are other program configurations as well, such as "newcomer classes" designed for immigrant students new to the country and "pull-out ELD or ESL classes," where students go with an ELD/ESL teacher for a period during the school day. These types of approaches can coexist with or augment other programs such as English immersion. (See Genesee, 1999, for a full description of these and other program alternatives for English learners.)

But what sorts of instructional environments are ELLs *actually* in? The question is difficult to answer, partly because of inconsistencies from state to state in how terms and programs are defined and reported. As shown in Figure 1.2, according to a 2001–2002 survey, 60 percent of English learners are in essentially all-English instruction: A fifth of these students—about 12 percent of all ELLs—are in all-English instruction and apparently receive no services or support at all related to their limited English proficiency

**Figure 1.2**  Instructional Language for ELLs

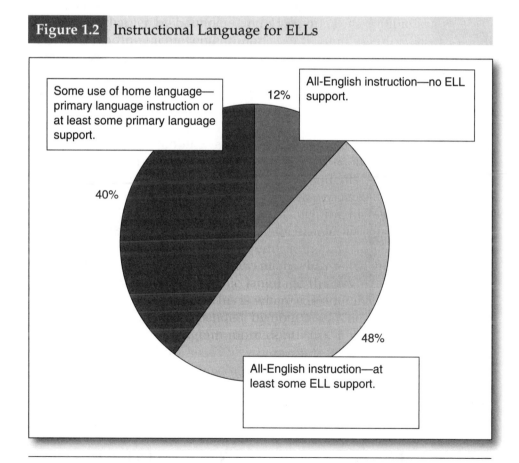

Some use of home language—primary language instruction or at least some primary language support.

12%

All-English instruction—no ELL support.

40%

48%

All-English instruction—at least some ELL support.

*Note:* Percentages are approximations, and there is wide variability within each segment. "All-English instruction—at least some ELL support" might be an overestimate since "All-English instruction—no ELL support" is probably illegal. See text for further details.

*Source:* Zehler, Fleischman, Hopstock, Stephenson, Pendzick, & Sapru, 2003.

(Zehler et al., 2003). This figure might actually be an underestimate. It comes from school and district officials who could be reluctant to report that ELLs receive "no services," which is likely to be a violation of the 1974 Supreme Court decision in *Lau v. Nichols* (414 U.S. No. 72–6520, pp. 563–572) requiring schools to teach ELLs so that they have "a meaningful opportunity to participate in the public educational program" (p. 563).

The rest of ELLs in all-English instruction receive some amount of "LEP (limited English proficient, a term formerly used more widely for ELLs and still used in federal and some state statutes and regulations) services," which can include the use of aides or resource teachers, instruction in ESL or ELD, or content instruction specially designed for students with limited English proficiency. The remaining ELLs—about 40 percent—are in programs that make some use of their home language. Here again there is a wide range, with nothing being typical. In some cases, students receive one of several forms of bilingual education, such as the models identified earlier (transitional, developmental, or dual language). In other cases, students are taught academic content in English, and their primary language is used only for support (e.g., translations by an aide, explanations during or after class, or to preview material prior to an all-English lesson). Currently, there is no way to know the amount of home language support students receive or, most critically, the quality of the instruction and whether it promotes achievement.

What we do know is that on average, ELLs' academic achievement is much too low. On state and national tests, students who are learning English consistently underperform in comparison to their English-speaking peers (see Goldenberg, 2008, for statistics and further references). These discrepancies should be no surprise since ELLs are limited in their English proficiency, and the tests used to gauge their progress are typically in English. But there is no way to know whether ELLs tested in English score low because of lagging content knowledge and skills, limited English proficiency, other factors that interfere with their test performance—or some combination. Whatever the explanation, we must do a better job of providing English learners with the educational opportunities they deserve. As part of this effort, teachers, administrators, other school staff, and policy makers must understand the state of our knowledge regarding the achievement of these students—what we can claim we know and where we are lacking credible information. The purpose of this book is to describe this knowledge base, as clearly and comprehensively as possible.

## A WORD ABOUT RESEARCH AND STATISTICS

Our goal in this book is to provide an accessible account of the research base on English learners. We are writing for educators and policy makers, not researchers, so we try to keep arcane matters of research and theory at arm's length. Unfortunately, much of what we can claim as "knowledge" is inextricably tied up with technical issues having to do with how research is conducted and the sorts of conclusions that certain studies or types of research permit. Therefore, we cannot completely avoid discussion of these issues. In order to not bog down the narrative, we will here go into some detail on two key methodological issues about which readers should be aware: first, the difference between correlation and causation; second, the problem of hidden influences, technically referred to as *confounds*. When these issues become relevant in one of the chapters, we will refer readers back to this section.

## Correlation and Causation

Many people recognize that correlation is not causation. In other words, just because two things (variables) go together does not mean one causes the other. Nonetheless, people—researchers included—routinely interpret correlations as demonstrating or implying a cause-and-effect relationship. Take, for example, the correlation between red wine and health. It turns out that drinking a glass or two of red wine each day is associated (that is, *correlated*) with health and longevity: People who drink moderate amounts of red wine have a lower risk of death. While many of us would like to interpret this association to mean that drinking red wine *causes* one to be healthier and live longer, in fact this has never been demonstrated. It is just as likely—and equally supported by the research since the data are all correlational—that healthier people also tend to drink moderate amounts of red wine. In other words, the wine itself might have no impact on health. It might be the other way around: Being healthy leads one to enjoy life more and imbibe a moderate amount of wine. As a recent *New York Times*[2] article reported,

> No study has ever proved a causal link between moderate drinking and a lower risk of death. . . . Moderate drinking may just be something healthy people tend to do, not something that makes people healthy.

More to the point of this book, consider English oral language proficiency and reading achievement in English (we take up this topic in Chapter 3, "Literacy Instruction in a Second Language"). To no one's surprise, the two are correlated: the better your English oral language skills, the better your English reading proficiency. But the question is, why? One presumably obvious explanation is that oral language proficiency

---

[2]*New York Times,* June 21, 2009. "Revised Wisdom, June 14–20." Available at http://tinyurl .com/mcrn4r.

"causes" or helps promote reading competence; the better you can speak and understand a language, the better you will be able to read it and understand what you are reading. Conversely, the weaker your command of the oral language, the poorer your ability to read it.

But it could well be that once you get past a certain level of oral language proficiency, more oral language proficiency does not *cause* or *promote* better English reading achievement. Instead, the opposite might be true: Being a better reader might help make you a better speaker (and listener). Competent reading in English helps you learn more of the language, thereby promoting more advanced English oral language skills (e.g., vocabulary, narrative skills). As with the correlation between drinking wine and being healthy, the cause and effect could also go both ways—oral proficiency promotes reading proficiency and reading proficiency promotes oral proficiency. Or, alternatively, neither causes the other, and instead both are the result of some common underlying language ability, which shows up in tests of oral language and reading proficiency.

The point is that the correlation itself says nothing about the direction of effect, that is, what causes what. It only tells you that two things—in this case, oral English proficiency and English reading proficiency—tend to go together (or in research speak, they "co-occur"). This distinction between correlation and causation is very important, since people want to draw practice and policy implications from correlations, but unless you know "what causes what" your practice or policy might have it backward or only partly right.

## Hidden Possible Influences
### (Technically, *Confounding Variables*)

Let's say students who are in Program A do better on achievement measures than do students in Program B. The first thing that comes to mind is that Program A works better. But what if Program A for some reason tends to have more students from higher-socioeconomic-status (SES) homes? We already know that SES and achievement are correlated (although, as discussed above, correlation does not mean causation, and we don't know exactly *why* the two are correlated), so the achievement difference between Program A and Program B students might have nothing to do with the program itself. Instead it might be the result of Program A's having more students with higher SES, and these students, on average, tend to score higher on achievement tests.

In the field of language-minority research this problem shows up, but as is true in other fields of educational research, it is often not recognized. ELLs attend different types of language programs, such as English immersion, transitional bilingual education, two-way bilingual education, and so forth (described briefly earlier in this chapter). People have compared the academic performance of students in different types of programs, and based on this, concluded which one works better. This seems reasonable enough until we consider that students who attend different types of programs might come from different types of families or differ from each other in ways that might influence their academic performance. For example, ELLs who attend two-way bilingual education programs (the goal of which is to promote bilingualism, biculturalism, and biliteracy) might come from homes where parents have somewhat higher education or have been in the United States longer or who speak more English to their children. We have in fact found this to be the case in research one of us has conducted (Goldenberg, 2006). These factors can very well affect children's academic achievement, irrespective of the program they are in. Or perhaps the two-way programs are deemed more challenging, and students who are less capable academically are either not placed in these programs or, if they are, tend to be removed if they are having academic difficulty. This too will affect comparisons between two-way programs and other programs.

The possibility of these hidden confounds is why "random assignment experiments" are usually considered the gold standard, that is, the preferred methodology for determining whether Program A (e.g., two-way immersion) works better than Program B (e.g., English immersion or transitional bilingual education). In a random assignment experiment, students are randomly assigned to a program. This makes it is less likely that subtle selection factors, known as *confounds*, can creep in and influence achievement, which in turn leads to erroneous conclusions about the relative effects of the programs. If there are differences between Program A and Program B students in a well-controlled and fully randomized experiment, we can be pretty confident that the differences are due to the program and not to a confounding factor.

Sometimes random assignment is not possible; in fact, random assignment is often not possible in schools. In this case, researchers will choose students who are already in different classrooms or schools and are either receiving different types of programs or are selected to receive different programs that will be compared. Aside from receiving different programs, these students should be as similar as possible to each other. This is sometimes called a *quasi-experiment*, since it is not quite a true experiment with randomization and other experimental controls. It is not ideal, since there could be hidden differences that do not show up until later. But at least if students are nearly identical in as many respects as possible, including their achievement before beginning the program, there is a greater chance that the comparison between programs will be valid.

The foregoing is generally important to keep in mind, since there are very few randomized studies in this research base, and to a surprising degree, researchers have not dealt directly with confounding variables. But this issue is also important for understanding one of the principle differences between conclusions reached by the NLP and the

CREDE reports. As we discuss in Chapter 2, the NLP concluded that although primary-language instruction ("bilingual education") has a positive effect on achievement *in English*, there was no basis for determining whether more time spent in primary-language instruction over a greater number of years produces better results than fewer years of primary-language instruction. The CREDE report, in contrast, concluded that more years in primary-language instruction leads to better results.

Yet regardless of the methodological complexities and nuances, the two reports converge on most findings and together contain considerable important information that we hope to help bring to a larger audience. We are convinced that students, educators, families, communities, and the country as a whole will be better served if educators know the contents of these reports and design policies and practices mindful of this content. But we must also recognize that there are big gaps in our understanding, as well as many unresolved issues and questions. We cannot shy away from this recognition; to the contrary, it is only by distinguishing among what we can say with some confidence, what we really have no good evidence for, and on what matters we have limited or imperfect understanding that we can make continued progress in enhancing educational opportunities for English learners. Absent this recognition, policy and practice will forever be subject to politics and predilections exclusively. Politics and predilections will always be with us in education, since education is never just about data. But valid and reliable data can help us practice better politics and inform our predilections.

## THE BOOK'S PLAN

Each of the next six chapters deals with a major topic in the education of ELLs. Chapter 2 discusses what we know about using ELLs' home language in their academic program; this is where we go into the bilingual education question, which has been so controversial for so long. In Chapter 3, we address learning to read in a language you are simultaneously learning to speak and understand; this is what happens when ELLs do not have primary-language instruction and instead—as is the case for most ELLs—are in what is sometimes called "English immersion." Chapter 4 deals with learning to speak and understand English per se, an obviously very important part of these students' educational agenda. Chapter 5 is somewhat parallel to Chapter 3, which deals exclusively with literacy; Chapter 5 discusses academic instruction in English for areas of the curriculum aside from literacy. Chapters 6 and 7 address topics outside of the classroom. Chapter 6 discusses school- and district-level factors that have a bearing on ELLs' achievement; Chapter 7 takes on sociocultural factors, including the influence of families, primarily parents. Each of Chapters 2–7 ends with our recommendations, based on our reading of the research or our "best guesses" when there is insufficient research. Finally, in Chapter 8, we attempt to synthesize across the chapters by presenting several illustrative scenarios, versions of which are also in individual chapters. We conclude with some suggestions for a broad framework to improve the academic achievement of students who come to school not speaking English well or even at all.

A note about citations in the text: When citing conclusions from the NLP (August & Shanahan, 2006) or CREDE (Genesee et al., 2006), we typically cite the reports rather than individual studies the reports reviewed. We cite individual studies when we discuss them in detail. More generally, we have attempted to keep in-text citations (e.g., "August & Shanahan, 2006") to a minimum to avoid distracting readers who are not interested in this level of detail.

# REFERENCES

Abedi, J. (Ed.). (2007). *English language proficiency assessment in the nation: Current status and future practice.* Davis: University of California, Davis.

Abedi, J. (2008). Classification system for English language learners: Issues and recommendations. *Educational Measurement: Issues and Practice, 27*(3), 17–31.

August, D., & Shanahan, T. (Eds.). (2006). *Developing literacy in second-language learners: Report of the National Literacy Panel on language-minority children and youth.* Mahwah, NJ: Lawrence Erlbaum.

Capps, R., Fix, M., Murray, J., Passel, J. S., & Herwantoro, S. (2005). *The new demography of America's schools: Immigration and the No Child Left Behind Act.* Washington, DC: The Urban Institute.

Carter, T. (1970). *Mexican Americans in school: A history of educational neglect.* New York: College Entrance Examination Board.

Carter, T., & Segura, R. (1979). *Mexican Americans in school: A decade of change.* New York: College Entrance Examination Board.

Coleman, R. (2006). *The role of school districts in the selection and support of English language development programs and approaches.* Unpublished doctoral dissertation, University of Southern California, Los Angeles.

Crawford, J. (2004). *Educating English learners: Language diversity in the classroom* (5th ed.). Los Angeles: Bilingual Education Services.

CTB McGraw-Hill. (2005). *Technical report for the California English Language Development Test (CELDT) 2003–2004 form C.* Monterey, CA: Author.

Cummins, J. (2009). Literacy and English-language learners: A shifting landscape for students, teachers, researchers, and policy makers. *Educational Researcher, 38*(5), 382–384.

Dutro, S. (2003). *A focused approach to English language instruction: A teacher's handbook.* San Diego, CA: California Reading and Literature Project.

Gándara, P., & Rumberger, R. (2006). *Resource needs for California's English learners.* Santa Barbara, CA: UC Linguistic Minority Research Institute. Retrieved from http://irepp.stanford.edu/documents/GDF/SUMMARIES/Gandara.pdf.

Genesee, F. (Ed). (1999). *Program alternatives for linguistically diverse students* (Educational Practice Report 1). Santa Cruz, CA: Center for Research on Education, Diversity & Excellence.

Genesee, F., Lindholm-Leary, K., Saunders, W., & Christian, D. (2006). *Educating English language learners.* New York: Cambridge University Press.

Goldenberg, C. (2006). *Family contexts and the language and literacy achievement of Spanish-speaking children.* Paper presented at the International Reading Association Annual Convention, Chicago, IL.

Goldenberg, C. (2008). Teaching English language learners: What the research does—and does not—say. *American Educator, 32*(2), 8–23, 42–44.

Kindler, A. (2002). *Survey of the states' limited English proficient students and available educational programs and services, 2000–2001 summary report.* Washington, DC: U.S. Department of Education. Accessed 9/10/09 from http://www .ncela.gwu.edu/files/rcd/BE021853/Survey_of_the_States.pdf.

Marcus, N., Adger, C. T., & Arteagoitia, I. (2007). *Registering students from language backgrounds other than English* (Issues & Answers Report, REL 2007–No. 025). Washington, DC: U.S. Department of Education, Institute of Education Sciences, National Center for Education Evaluation and Regional Assistance, Regional Educational Laboratory Appalachia. Retrieved from http://ies.ed.gov/ncee/edlabs.

Natriello, G., McDill, E., & Pallas, A. (1990). *Schooling disadvantaged students: Racing against catastrophe.* New York: Teachers College Press.

Planty, M., Hussar, W., Snyder, T., Kena, G., KewalRamani, A., Kemp, J., et al. (2009). *The condition of education 2009* (NCES 2009–081). Washington, DC: U.S. Department of Education National Center for Education Statistics, Institute of Education Sciences.

Pray, L., & Jiménez, R. (2009). Literacy and English-language learners: What researchers and policy makers should know. *Educational Researcher, 38*(5), 380–381.

Rodriguez, R. (1982). *Hunger of memory: The education of Richard Rodriguez.* New York: Bantam Books.

Schleppegrell, M., Greer, S., & Taylor, S. (2008). Literacy in history: Language and meaning. *Australian Journal of Language and Literacy, 31,* 174–187.

Sirin, S. (2005). Socioeconomic status and academic achievement: A meta-analytic review of research. *Review of Educational Research, 75,* 417–453.

Stokes-Guinan, K., & Goldenberg, C. (in press). California English language development test, or CELDT: Strengths, weaknesses, and issues for consideration. *California Association of Teachers of English to Speakers of Other Languages (CATESOL) Journal.*

Zehler, A. M., Fleischman, H. L., Hopstock, P. J., Stephenson, T. G., Pendzick, M. L., & Sapru, S. (2003). *Descriptive study of services to LEP students and LEP students with disabilities.* Volume I: *Research Report.* Arlington, VA: Development Associates.

# 2

## *The Role of the Home Language*

The role of the home language in the education of English learners—the so-called bilingual education question—has historically been *the* big issue in this field. Certainly there are many other important factors to consider, not least of which is the quality of instruction regardless of *language* of instruction. Fortunately, we are seeing increased research addressing these other issues. But the bilingual education question has so dominated the field for so long,

- What are the commonly held views about instructing ELLs in their primary (home) language, often called "bilingual education"?
- What does research say about the effectiveness of primary-language instruction?
- Can students learn English literacy skills while learning to read in their primary language?
- Can ELLs' primary language still play a role in their instruction even if they are in English immersion? If so, what?
- What are possible advantages of two-way bilingual education?

that it makes sense to begin here. In essence the question is this: Should students who come to school speaking a language other than English be instructed exclusively in English or in some combination of their home language (sometimes called the "primary language" or L1) and English (L2)? The issue has generated enormous controversy, and bilingual programs have attracted frequent attacks and criticisms for many reasons.

On a political and ideological level, many individuals object to a language other than English being used in school (unless it's being taught as a foreign language) for the supposedly simple reason that English is the most common language in the United States and should be the language used for school instruction. English is certainly the predominant language in the United States, as a result of migrations, wars, annexations, trade, choices, impositions, and, ultimately, sheer number of speakers. But the country does not have an official language. Speakers of hundreds of languages—including the many languages spoken by native Indians long before the Europeans and their dozen or so languages arrived—have inhabited what is now the United States. Nevertheless, many argue that English is the de facto official language of the United States and should be the language of laws, commerce, administration, and, of course, education. Some observers worry that sanctioning multiple languages and multiple cultures will lead to a *dis*uniting of the United States (e.g., Schlesinger, 1998). But political and ideological arguments come from different perspectives. There are also forceful proponents of bilingual education who contend that, at bottom, opposition to primary-language instruction is always motivated by political, ideological, and even racial issues.

A different objection is not against bilingual education itself, so much as the way it is sometimes implemented. Educators and parents alike have expressed concern when a child, attending a school since kindergarten, is still at an intermediate proficiency level in fifth grade. The concern here is not with bilingual education as designed, but that some programs turned out to be monolingual Spanish or monolingual English programs. Sometimes students were not receiving enough formal or informal English instruction. "What is not being voiced in the same breath," Villarreal and Solis (1998) noted, "is that effective bilingual education programs are not to blame but rather shortages in qualified teachers and poorly constructed programs."

A third set of objections to the use of the home language is fueled less by ideological concerns and more by pragmatic educational ones. Here, the question is whether children who are instructed in the home language will be deprived of sufficient exposure to English, thereby slowing their English acquisition and delaying entry into the educational mainstream. Critics of bilingual education from this perspective argue that the best way to learn a second language is to be immersed in it, as early and intensively as possible. Anything short of this, they argue, simply wastes precious time that English learners need to become proficient in English as efficiently as possible.

## COMMON SENSE DOES NOT NECESSARILY LEAD TO TRUTH

It's understandable how people can take this perspective. A few years ago a fair-minded colleague expressed disbelief to one of us about bilingual education: "Doesn't it just make sense," she asked, trying to understand an issue that seems to confound many people, "that the earlier and more intensively children are placed in all-English instruction the better their English achievement will eventually be? Doesn't it just make *sense*?" From most people's standpoint, bilingual education probably does *not* make sense. It seems so illogical: How can spending more time receiving instruction in one language (e.g., Spanish) produce as good or better results in another language (e.g., English)? It does seem contrary to common sense.

But this is why we do scientific research. Common sense does not always turn out to be the best guide to truth. If we only relied on common sense, we would still think the sun revolves around the earth, that you can't get east by heading west, and that added weight makes objects fall faster.

As it turns out, the best scientific studies we have—those that control for extraneous variables and provide the most confidence in their conclusions—show that in fact using students' *primary language* (L1) promotes their achievement in English (their L2). Several dozen studies have been conducted and reported over the past 35 years attempting to compare the results of teaching children to read in their home language to teaching them to read only in their second language (such as English). Some of these studies were experiments; others were not. As we discussed in Chapter 1, experimental studies are considered the gold standard if one wants to determine the effect of a particular program or type of instruction. Experiments use treatment and comparison groups, as well as other controls designed to ensure that any impacts found can be attributed to the treatment, instead of to extraneous factors such as differences between two groups of students. There are problems with conducting such studies, to be sure. They are difficult to carry out, there are ethical issues, and there is the practical reality that students move around or their parents can change their program, thus wreaking havoc with a supposedly "controlled" study. Nonetheless, as a general rule, experiments provide a stronger basis than other types of studies for making claims about the effects of one program or another.

The consensus—although it is not unanimous—among the experimental studies of primary-language instruction is that teaching ELLs to read in their home language in fact boosts their achievement in the second language, as compared to teaching them only in their second language. By far the most compelling research in this area is with respect to learning to read. Although it is likely that primary-language instruction is also beneficial in other curriculum areas, such as math, social studies, and science, the research is not nearly as strong.

To date, five separate meta-analyses (or "quantitative syntheses") have reached essentially the same conclusion about the benefits of teaching children to read in their home language. (Box 2.1 lists these syntheses.) A meta-analysis is a statistical technique that allows researchers to combine data from many studies and estimate the average effect of an instructional procedure. Meta-analyses are useful because studies often come to conflicting conclusions. Some find positive effects of a program, others find negative effects of the same type of program, and yet others find no effects. Even among studies that report positive findings, the effects can be small or large. A meta-analysis addresses these questions: *Overall*, is the average effect of a particular practice positive, negative, or zero? And if the average effect is positive or negative, is the *magnitude* of the effect large and therefore meaningful? Small and therefore of little consequence? Or something in between?

---

**Box 2.1**

**The Five Quantitative Syntheses That Concluded Primary-Language Instruction Promotes Achievement in *English* (in chronological order)**

- Willig, A. (1985). A meta-analysis of selected studies on the effectiveness of bilingual education. *Review of Educational Research, 55*, 269–317.
- Greene, J. (1997). A meta-analysis of the Rossell and Baker review of bilingual education research. *Bilingual Research Journal, 21*, 103–122.
- Rolstad, K. Mahoney, K., & Glass, G. (2005). The big picture: A meta-analysis of program effectiveness research on English language learners. *Educational Policy, 19*, 572–594.
- Slavin, R., & Cheung, A. (2005). A synthesis of research on language of reading instruction for English language learners. *Review of Educational Research, 75*, 247–281.
- Francis, D., Lesaux, N., & August, D. (2006). Language of instruction. In D. August & T. Shanahan (Eds.), *Developing literacy in second-language learners: Report of the National Literacy Panel on language-minority children and youth* (pp. 365–413). Mahwah, NJ: Lawrence Erlbaum.

---

The National Literacy Panel (NLP) conducted the latest of these five meta-analyses (Francis et al., 2006), all of which reached the same conclusion about the positive effects of teaching children to read in their home language. The other four meta-analyses were reported by Greene (1997), Rolstad et al. (2005), Slavin and Cheung (2005), and Willig (1985). Following a finding first reported by Slavin and Cheung (Slavin was originally on the NLP but resigned to publish his review separately), the NLP reported that in some of the studies, students learned to read in their home language and in the second language simultaneously, although at different times of the day. This suggests that instead of students' having to learn to read in the home language first, and only then learning to read in the second language (the typical bilingual education model), they can learn to read in both simultaneously. Aside from this important new insight, the results of the five meta-analyses have been remarkably consistent. Readers should understand how unusual it is even to have five meta-analyses on the same issue conducted by five independent researchers or groups of researchers with diverse perspectives. The fact that they all reached essentially the same conclusion is extraordinary. In fact, the benefits of teaching ELLs to read in their primary language might be one of the strongest findings in the entire field of educational research. Period.

Let's be clear: The effects of primary-language instruction are real, but they are modest. Researchers gauge the effect of a program or an instructional practice in terms of an "effect size," which tells us how much improvement can be expected from using the program or practice. The average effect size of primary-language reading instruction over two to three years (the typical length of time children in the studies were followed) is around .35–.40; estimates range from about .20 to about .60, depending on how the calculation is done. What does this mean? It means that teaching students to read in their home language can boost reading achievement in the second language by a total of about 12–15 percentile points over two to three years. Translation: Say you have two highly comparable groups of students, one taught to read in Spanish and the other taught to read in English—that is, this latter group is learning to speak and understand the language as they are learning to read and write in it. After two to three years, you can expect that the average (or "median") student learning to read in Spanish—that is, the student who scores exactly at the middle of the group receiving Spanish literacy instruction—will have higher achievement than 62 to 65 percent of the students in the group receiving all-English instruction. This is what an effect size of .35–.40 translates into. These effects apply to elementary as well as secondary students (although only 2 of the 17 studies the NLP included in the meta-analysis were with secondary students, both produced positive effects).

This magnitude of effect is not huge, but neither is it trivial. To provide some perspective, the National Reading Panel (2000), which reviewed experimental research on English speakers only, found that the average effect size of phonics instruction is .44, a bit larger than the likely average effect size of primary-language reading instruction. Primary-language reading instruction is clearly no panacea, just as phonics instruction is no panacea. But relatively speaking, it makes a meaningful contribution to ELLs' reading achievement *in English*. The scenario in Box 2.2 illustrates a program where Spanish-speaking ELLs learn to read in their home language as they also learn oral and academic skills and content in English. More detailed information and scenarios about different program options for ELLs can be found in Genesee (1999).

## Box 2.2

### Primary-Language Early Literacy Program

In Grades K–2 at Las Palmas Elementary, language arts and math instruction for Spanish-speaking ELLs is in Spanish. Science and social studies are taught in Spanish in kindergarten and the beginning of first grade; by the second half of first grade, teachers use sheltered instruction and content-based ELD (English Language Development; see Chapters 4 and 5) to teach science and social studies concepts and English simultaneously. Students have art, music, and PE in English. They receive at least 45 minutes per day of dedicated ELD (Chapter 4), geared to students' proficiency levels, from the time they enter the school.

Children at Las Palmas typically transition to all-English instruction by the third grade. But in Grades K–2, the school has a rigorous Spanish literacy program where students become proficient Spanish readers within two years as they learn academic content (in English and Spanish) and develop their English language skills.

Ms. L's language arts lessons are identical to grade-level language arts lessons anywhere, except that they are in Spanish. Actually, they are relatively more advanced than typical language arts lessons in second grade since children who learn to read in Spanish can learn more quickly (due to the simpler Spanish orthography) and therefore can read virtually any Spanish written text. Las Palmas's Spanish reading program is structured and explicit; most children master the skills of reading, and can read with considerable fluency, by Grade 2.

In addition, the meta-analyses found that bilingual education helps ELLs become bilingual and biliterate. Knowing two languages confers numerous obvious advantages—cultural, intellectual, cognitive (see, e.g., Bialystock, 2001), vocational, and economic (some studies have found increased earnings for bilingual individuals; Saiz & Zoido, 2005). Interpretations must be made cautiously, however, since individuals become bilingual in different ways and under different circumstances. Because of all the possible hidden confounds (see Chapter 1), we cannot say with certainty that the advantages observed among relatively advantaged bilingual individuals such as those studied by Bialystock and Saiz and Zoido also would be observed among individuals in bilingual programs for ELLs. Nonetheless, the considerable possible advantages of bilingualism per se should be part of the discussion about bilingual education in this country. All too often, unfortunately, the debate is solely about learning and becoming academically proficient in English. As undoubtedly important as English proficiency is, we should broaden the discussion and think about the benefits of bilingualism and biliteracy.

# DIFFERENCES BETWEEN
# THE NLP AND CREDE REPORTS

The Center for Research on Education, Diversity and Excellence (CREDE) report also concluded that primary-language instruction was beneficial, but its methods and conclusions were different in important respects from the NLP's. First, the CREDE report was a research review, not a meta-analysis. Instead of attempting to determine the "average" effect of primary-language instruction, CREDE researchers considered many of the studies of instructional language and drew conclusions based on sifting through and weighing the evidence. Second, the NLP's meta-analysis only included studies that were either random assignment experiments or involved students already in different programs but very similar in other respects, whereas the CREDE report did not use such strict criteria for selecting studies. Finally, while the NLP only considered literacy outcomes (primarily reading), the CREDE report considered the impact on instructional language in all areas of the curriculum.

While both reports concluded that primary-language instruction makes a positive contribution to the academic achievement of ELLs, there were two issues where the findings differed.

First, the CREDE report concluded that more years of primary-language instruction produced better results; the NLP report said there were insufficient data to reach any conclusion on the matter. The reason for this discrepancy is that the studies that met the NLP's stricter methodological criteria typically lasted two to three years. No long-term studies met the criteria, so it was impossible to make meaningful distinctions as to the length of time students received bilingual instruction. Within the studies' relatively narrow time band, there were no differences in the effects of primary-language instruction based on the length of time students received primary-language instruction. One of the five meta-analyses we discussed previously (Rolsad et al., 2005) concluded that more years of primary-language instruction were more beneficial for English achievement; the other four (including the NLP) came to no conclusion about length of time.

One of the studies excluded by the NLP but included in the CREDE report was a very influential one by Wayne Thomas and Virginia Collier (2002), itself a replication of a prior and even more influential report, also by Thomas and Collier (1997). The two Thomas and Collier reports and several program evaluations of two-way bilingual programs (most notably those conducted by Kathryn Lindholm-Leary), considered the effect of different language programs over a much longer time period than the studies reviewed by the NLP. Thomas and Collier (2002), for example, included data on students in Grades 5, 8, and 11 who had been in programs that used the primary language either extensively or not at all. But these studies did not control for preexisting or population differences. It is entirely plausible that programs providing primary-language instruction for five, six, or more years (e.g., two-way bilingual education) obtain even better results than programs that use it for only a short time. Moreover, there is some evidence of two-way bilingual programs' fostering positive cross-cultural and bilingual attitudes among students (Lindholm-Leary, 2001), which clearly can be considered a positive outcome. The scenario in Box 2.3 illustrates a two-way program. (See Genesee, 1999, for more detailed information and scenarios.) However, the evidence is not as compelling as it is for the more general finding that L1 reading instruction boosts L2 reading achievement.

## Box 2.3

### Two-Way or Dual Immersion

Emory Ave. Elementary School uses a "50/50" dual immersion model—children receive half of their instruction in English and half in Spanish. Mr. F. and Ms. D. teach fourth grade, and their classrooms are next door to each other. Each has a class that is evenly split between students from Spanish-speaking homes and those who are English speakers (mostly Anglos but also a few African Americans).

In the early grades children learn to read and write in both languages. They learn science, PE, and art in English and social studies and music in Spanish. In later years they switch and learn science, PE, and art in Spanish and social studies and music in English, so that over the years children receive instruction in both languages in all content areas. There is always a designated Spanish teacher and a designated English teacher for each subject. Teachers work in two-person teams, sometimes supplemented by an art, music, or PE "specialist," and they exchange students during instructional periods. In the early grades, one teacher teaches beginning and early English reading to the English speakers in both classrooms while the partner teaches beginning and early Spanish reading to the Spanish speakers. Later in the day they switch, and the English speakers get Spanish reading; the Spanish speakers get English reading. Most of the day is spent in mixed language groups. For example, one teacher will teach science in English to half of his class and half of his partner's class (mixed English and Spanish group) while the partner teaches social studies to the rest of the children in Spanish; they switch on alternate days.

While the goals of the program are high levels of literacy, academic achievement, and language proficiency in both English and Spanish, the program also has explicit social goals: It aims to integrate children from different language and cultural backgrounds, with neither language nor culture seen as dominant or superior. Cultural awareness and appreciation are thus very important aspects of the whole-school program, and these are reflected in activities and lessons in Mr. F.'s and Ms. D.'s classrooms. Art, music, literature, customs, and historical and contemporary personages from the Anglo and Latino American worlds are amply represented.

The second major difference between the two reports is that while the NLP only considered reading outcomes (e.g., word reading, comprehension, reading vocabulary, total reading), the CREDE report also discussed math, writing, and science outcomes and considered the effects of instructional language on other outcomes such as grades, attendance, grade retention, and high school graduation. Reading outcomes were by far the most numerous, since that is the variable that has been most studied. But the other results were consistent with those for reading: positive effects for home language instruction and even more positive effects the longer students were in a program that continued to use the primary language in addition to using English. Again, it is highly plausible that what is true for reading outcomes is also true for other academic outcomes, but the evidence is not as strong.

# HOW TO EXPLAIN EFFECTS OF
# L1 INSTRUCTION ON L2 ACHIEVEMENT?

One possible key to understanding how primary-language instruction results in higher achievement in English is what educational psychologists and cognitive scientists call *transfer*. Transfer is one of the most venerable and important concepts in education. In the simplest terms, transfer means that what you learn in one context or setting influences what you know, can do, and can learn in another context or setting. Without transfer, nothing we learn in school would really matter since it could not be applied or used anywhere but in school and in the particular context in which it was learned. We would all literally be helpless without transfer. With respect to English learners, a substantial body of research reviewed by both the CREDE and NLP reports suggests (although conclusive proof is hard to come by) that literacy and other skills and knowledge transfer across languages. That is, if you learn something in one language—such as decoding skills, comprehension strategies, or a concept such as democracy—either you already know it in (i.e., transfer it to) the other language, or you can more easily learn it in the other language. The reader brings not only linguistic knowledge to bear on the task of reading but also world knowledge and topical knowledge (Pearson, 2006) that is essential for reading comprehension. Background knowledge acquired in the first language probably facilitates comprehension when reading in the second language.

Another possible explanation for L1 to L2 effects that is related to transfer, but not exactly the same thing, is the concept of "underlying proficiency," coined and popularized by Jim Cummins. What this means is that reading instruction (or other academic instruction) in one language contributes to a general proficiency (in reading or in other academic domains) that then helps boost learning and achievement when students learn to read (or receive other academic instruction) in another language. Yet another possibility, more recently proposed by Bransford and Schwartz (1998), is that all learning influences "preparedness for future learning," that is, learning sort of "primes the pump" or otherwise makes us more ready to learn or disposed to learning more. So the more an ELL learns in L1, the more prepared she will be for additional learning, whether in L1 or L2.

Theoretical fine points aside, what the experimental studies showing L1 instruction's effects on L2 achievement demonstrate is that the presumed common sense of "more time in English will produce better outcomes in English" does not quite pan out. Being able to read in a particular language requires two things: learning (or knowing how) to read and learning (or knowing) the language. While learning the language undoubtedly requires spending enough time learning, listening to, and practicing that language, learning to read requires a different type of learning, which we will discuss in more detail in the next chapter, dealing with literacy specifically.

In brief, becoming a proficient reader requires learning concepts such as that speech is made up of sounds, and these sounds are represented by letters; when letter sounds are combined, they forms words; words form phrases, sentences, and longer texts; comprehending texts requires fluent word recognition, knowledge of the words and concepts in the texts, and the use of certain reading strategies. All of these are accomplished more readily and efficiently in a language one already knows. Then, given adequate instruction, opportunity, and exposure, these skills and understandings will transfer to a second language (or create an underlying literacy proficiency; or prepare the student for future learning in L2, depending on your preferred theoretical explanation). The key point is that this time spent learning to read in L1 is not time wasted. To the contrary: It makes a direct contribution to achievement in L2, assuming L2 learning opportunities are adequate.

However, teachers cannot assume that transfer (or application of proficiency) is automatic. Jiménez (1997) found that students sometimes do not realize that what they know in their first language (e.g., cognates such as *elefante* and *elephant* or *ejemplo* and *example*; or reading skills and strategies) can be applied in their second. Jiménez puts it this way: "Less successful bilingual readers view their two languages as separate and unrelated, and they often see their non-English language backgrounds as detrimental" (p. 227). Ideally, teachers should be aware of what students know and can do in their primary language so they can help them apply this knowledge and skill to tasks in English. The scenario in Box 2.4 illustrates the benefits of a strong primary-language program and the likely transfer to English of literacy skills learned in the first language.

---

**Box 2.4**

**Transfer From Primary Language to English Literacy**

Because of the strong Spanish reading program, Ms. L. can have most children read a range of stories, chapter books, poems, and nonfiction work. She focuses on reading comprehension, vocabulary, writing, discussions, and book reports. She also has students read a lot of nonfiction, especially about topics she will cover in her sheltered social studies and science instruction. She finds that when the students become familiar with topics by reading and discussing them in Spanish, they do much better during English instruction on those same topics.

When her students enter third grade in September, they will transition to an all-English program and will receive language arts instruction in English. The language arts transition program is specifically designed to help students build on their Spanish literacy skills and learn the more complex English orthography. Although many reading skills readily transfer from Spanish to English, students must learn about long and short vowels, irregular patterns, and numerous odd-ities of written English. Because students are fully literate in Spanish (at least those who have been in the school since kindergarten; late arrivals pose contin-ual challenges), they learn the English orthographic patterns and apply them to their reading and writing. It is not always easy, but in general, students catch on and become English literate within a couple of years. Students also continue to receive instruction in writing (mechanics and composition) and wide reading appropriate to their English reading levels.

---

Transfer of reading skills across languages appears to occur even if lan-guages use different alphabetic systems, although the different alphabets probably diminish the degree of transfer. For example, studies of transfer between English and Spanish find relatively high correlations on measures of word reading, phonological awareness, and spelling. Some studies of English and non-Roman alphabets (e.g., Arabic, Persian), in contrast, find much lower correlations. However, comprehension skills appear to trans-fer readily between languages with different alphabets, such as English and Korean (see Section II, "Cross-linguistic Relationships in Second-Language Learners," in August & Shanahan, 2006).

## STILL MANY UNKNOWNS

We still have more questions than answers about the role of the home lan-guage in the education of ELLs. With any luck, the CREDE and NLP reports will help make the case that the students' L1 can contribute to their education. We should use these reports to get beyond the old debates about whether bilingual education works and use them as catalysts to help untangle the role of the primary language and address critical questions about which we have essentially no research. For example, consider the following questions:

- Is primary-language instruction more beneficial for some learners than for others, such as those with weaker or stronger primary-language skills? Weaker or stronger English skills?
- Is L1 instruction more effective in some settings and with certain ELL populations than others?
- What should be the relative emphasis between promoting knowledge and skills in the primary language and developing English language proficiency?
- What level of skill in the students' primary language does the teacher need to possess to be effective?

We presently cannot answer these questions with confidence. Individual studies might point in certain directions, but we lack a body of solid research that permit us to go beyond the general finding about the positive effects of primary-language instruction on reading achievement in English.

## IS THERE A PLACE FOR L1 IN ENGLISH IMMERSION PROGRAMS?

A final important question about which we have little solid data is what role, if any, should the home language play in English immersion programs? Given that most ELLs are in essentially all-English programs, it is very relevant to ask whether the primary language has a role in these situations. The evidence we have so far suggests that it does. (See Box 2.5 for a list of possible L1 "supports" in English immersion.)

---

**Box 2.5**

### Primary-Language (L1) Supports in English Instruction

- Clarifications and explanations in L1
- Preview-review (teacher introduces, or "previews," new concepts in the primary language and then afterward reviews the new content, again in the primary language; lesson itself is taught all in English)
- Focusing on similarities and differences between L1 and English (e.g., cognates, orthographic features)
- Teaching a strategy in L1, followed by student applying it in English

Probably the most obvious possible way to use the primary language for instructional support is for clarification and explanation. This can be done by the teacher, a classroom aide, a peer, or a volunteer in the classroom. It is easy to see how explaining or clarifying concepts in the home language can help provide ELLs with access to what is going on in the classroom. But it is also not difficult to imagine downsides. For example, if peers provide the explanations, they might not be accurate; or students might become dependent on a "translator" who provides a crutch, resulting in students not exerting themselves to learn English; or if translations or periodic explanations in the primary language are offered throughout lessons, students can "tune out" during the English part (Legarreta, 1979; Legarreta-Marcaida, 1981). We have inadequate research on these topics— in particular, how any of these uses of the primary language in an English immersion context influences student achievement.

Another form of primary-language support, but one that keeps the focus on English instruction, is to introduce new concepts in the primary language prior to the lesson in English, then afterward review the new content, again in the primary language (sometimes called "preview-review"; see Ovando, Collier, & Combs, 2003). This is different from clarification and explanation since what this does is "frontload" the new learning in the student's primary language and then allows for review after the lesson. There is no ongoing explanation or translation. When the real lesson is delivered in English, the student already is somewhat familiar with the content, but he or she has to concentrate to get the message as it is delivered in English. Because of the previewing, the language used in the lesson should be more comprehensible and, in principle at least, the student will walk away knowing more content *and* more language (vocabulary, key phrases). Then by reviewing lesson content after the lesson, the teacher checks to see whether students accomplished the lesson objective. The NLP reviewed a study that provided some support for the effectiveness of this approach. Prior to reading a book in English, teachers previewed difficult vocabulary in the primary language (Spanish) and then afterward reviewed the material in Spanish. This produced better comprehension and recall than either of the two control conditions: reading the book in English or doing a simultaneous Spanish translation while reading.

Teachers can also offer primary-language support by focusing on the similarities and differences between English and students' native language. For example, if using the Roman alphabet, many letters represent the same sounds in English and other languages, but others do not. In addition, languages have cognates, that is, words with shared meanings from common etymological roots (*geography* and *geografia*, for instance). Calling students' attention to these cognates could help extend their vocabularies and improve their comprehension. However, we do not know the effect of cognate instruction per se. There are a number of useful sources of Spanish-English cognates that teachers of ELLs can consult (e.g., Calderón, August, Durán, Madden, Slavin, & Gil, 2003). Nash (1999) offers an exhaustive, book-length list, but also see Prado (1996) for false cognates that can cause problems, such as (our personal favorite) *embarrassed* and *embarazada*. The latter means *pregnant*. When used to refer to someone who is embarrassed, and especially when put in the masculine form—*embarazado*—it can really light up a classroom of Spanish-speaking adolescents.

A study not included in the NLP provides another example of how the primary language can be used to support learning in English. Fung, Wilkinson, and Moore (2003) found that introducing reciprocal teaching strategies in students' primary language improved reading comprehension in the second language. Reciprocal teaching is a technique for promoting reading comprehension where students are taught four strategies—asking questions about the text, summarizing what they have read, clarifying the text's meaning, and predicting what will come next. Fung et al. taught middle school ELLs reciprocal teaching strategies in their primary language and in English. They then found that students used more reading strategies *and* that their reading comprehension improved when they read in English. However, the study did not compare home-language-assisted reciprocal teaching with English-only reciprocal teaching; thus we do not really know the role primary-language support itself played in improving student comprehension.

Of course, in many schools the questions of how long and to what extent students' primary language should be used do not even arise. Neither primary-language instruction nor primary-language support is sometimes feasible, either because there is no qualified staff, because students come from numerous language backgrounds, or, sadly, because of uninformed policy choices or political decisions, such as California's Proposition 227. Proposition 227 passed in 1998 and has succeeded in drastically reducing primary-language instruction in California; but it has not delivered on its promised effects on ELL achievement (American Institutes for Research & WestEd, 2006). In any case, we do have research that can provide guidance on how to help English learners in all-English contexts. We turn to this in the following chapters.

## RECOMMENDATIONS

- **If at all possible, teach students literacy skills in their home language.** A number of studies have shown that teaching ELLs to read in their home language will boost their reading achievement in the second language while teaching them home-language literacy skills.
- **Students can be taught literacy skills in English while they are learning literacy skills in their home language.** Students are able to learn to read in both languages simultaneously, although instruction should occur at different times of the day.

- **Teaching ELLs subject matter content in their primary language might be beneficial.** This strategy is probably a more efficient way to promote content knowledge than teaching content in a language students do not understand well.
- **If possible, maintain primary-language instruction throughout elementary school or beyond, such as in two-way bilingual programs.** This will help develop literacy and academic skills in the primary language and might have positive effects on achievement in English and attitudes toward different languages and cultures.
- **Even in an all-English instructional environment, assess students' language, literacy, and academic skills in students' home language.** Teachers need to know what students know and can do in their primary language so they can help them consciously transfer the skills and knowledge from their home language to English.
- **Use L1 support in all-English classes to preview, clarify, and explain.** For example, new content and skills can be introduced and reviewed in the primary language before and after lessons are taught in English. However, direct translation is probably not helpful since students can tune out and wait for the translation.
- **Point out similarities (e.g., cognates) and differences (e.g., spelling patterns) between English and the primary language.** This probably helps ELLs transfer knowledge and skills from their first language to English.

# REFERENCES

American Institutes for Research & WestEd. (2006). *Effects of the implementation of Proposition 227 on the education of English learners, K–12: Findings from a five-year evaluation.* Washington, DC: American Institutes for Research.

August, D., & Shanahan, T. (Eds.). (2006). *Developing literacy in second-language learners: Report of the National Literacy Panel on language-minority children and youth.* Mahwah, NJ: Lawrence Erlbaum.

Bialystock, E. (2001). *Bilingualism in development: Language, literacy, and cognition.* New York: Cambridge University Press.

Bransford, J. D., & Schwartz, D. L. (1998). Rethinking transfer: A simple proposal with multiple implications. *Review of Research in Education, 24,* 61–100.

Calderón, M., August, D., Durán, D., Madden, N., Slavin, R., & Gil, M. (2003). *Spanish to English transitional reading: Teacher's manual.* Baltimore, MD: The Success for All Foundation. Adapted version available at www.ColorinColorado.org.

Francis, D., Lesaux, N., & August, D. (2006). Language of instruction. In D. August & T. Shanahan (Eds.), *Developing literacy in second-language learners: Report of the National Literacy Panel on language-minority children and youth* (pp. 365–413). Mahwah, NJ: Lawrence Erlbaum.

Fung, I., Wilkinson, I., & Moore, D. (2003). L1-assisted reciprocal teaching to improve ESL students' comprehension of English expository text. *Learning and Instruction, 13,* 1–31.

Genesee, F. (Ed). (1999). *Program alternatives for linguistically diverse students* (Educational Practice Report 1). Santa Cruz, CA: Center for Research on Education, Diversity & Excellence.

Greene, J. (1997). A meta-analysis of the Rossell and Baker review of bilingual education research. *Bilingual Research Journal, 21*, 103–122.

Jiménez, R. (1997). The strategic reading abilities and potential of five low-literacy Latina/o readers in middle school. *Reading Research Quarterly, 32*, 224–243.

Legarreta, D. (1979). The effects of program models on language acquisition by Spanish-speaking children. *TESOL Quarterly, 13*, 521–534.

Legarreta-Marcaida, D. (1981). Effective use of the primary language in the classroom. In California State Department of Education, *Schooling and language minority children* (pp. 83–116). Los Angeles: Evaluation, Dissemination and Assessment Center, California State University, Los Angeles.

Lindholm-Leary, K. (2001). *Dual language education.* Clevedon, UK: Multilingual Matters.

Nash, R. (1999). *Dictionary of Spanish cognates thematically organized.* Sylmar, CA: NTC.

National Reading Panel. (2000). *Report of the National Reading Panel—Teaching children to read: An evidence-based assessment of the scientific research literature on reading and its implications for reading instruction (report of the subgroups).* Washington, DC: National Institute of Child Health and Human Development. Retrieved from http://www.nichd.nih.gov/publications/nrp/report.cfm.

Ovando, C., Collier, V., & Combs, M. C. (2003). *Bilingual and ESL classrooms: Teaching in multicultural contexts* (3rd ed.). Boston: McGraw Hill.

Pearson, P. D. (2006). *A new framework for teaching comprehension.* Presentation given at Developing Tomorrow's Thinkers: Comprehension and Beyond, University of California Berkeley Summer Institute in Reading, Berkeley, CA.

Prado, M. (1996). *Dictionary of Spanish false cognates.* Sylmar, CA: NTC.

Rolstad, K., Mahoney, K., & Glass, G. (2005). The big picture: A meta-analysis of program effectiveness research on English language learners. *Educational Policy, 19*, 572–594.

Saiz, A., & Zoido, E. (2005). Listening to what the world says: Bilingualism and earnings in the United States. *Review of Economics and Statistics, 87*, 523–538.

Schlesinger, A. (1998). *The disuniting of America: Reflections on a multicultural society.* New York: Norton.

Slavin, R., & Cheung, A. (2005). A synthesis of research on language of reading instruction for English language learners. *Review of Educational Research, 75*, 247–281.

Thomas, W., & Collier, V. (1997). *School effectiveness for language minority students.* Washington, DC: National Clearinghouse for Bilingual Education. (ERIC Document Reproduction Service No. ED436087)

Thomas, W. P., & Collier, V. P. (2002). *A national study of school effectiveness for language minority students' long-term academic achievement.* Santa Cruz, CA: Center for Research on Education, Diversity & Excellence. http://www.cal.org/resources/digest/ResBrief10.html.

Villarreal, A., & Solis, A. (1998). In bilingual education. *IDRA Newsletter, 25*(1). http://www.idra.org/IDRA_Newsletter.

Willig, A. (1985). A meta-analysis of selected studies on the effectiveness of bilingual education. *Review of Educational Research, 55*, 269–317.

# 3

# *Literacy Instruction in a Second Language*

It's hard to deny how important literacy development is. Simply put, students need to read and write at sufficiently high levels if they are to be successful throughout school and beyond. Certainly individuals can have meaningful and satisfying lives without being excellent, or even very good, readers; conversely, one can be an outstanding reader but not be happy or successful in life. But while high levels of literacy don't guarantee anything, individuals' options are undeniably limited in direct relation to limited academic skills. Anyone who doubts this should consult any of a number of publications and reports dealing with the relationship between literacy skills and social, economic, and occupational success (e.g., Guthrie, Schafer, & Hutchinson, 1991; Kaestle, 1991; Miller, 1988; Murnane & Levy, 1996). The issue is particularly critical for ELLs, as we pointed out in the first chapter, because of

- What key components of English literacy for ELLs were examined by the National Literacy Panel?
- In what ways is literacy instruction for ELLs similar to literacy instruction for English speakers?
- In what ways is it different?
- What sorts of instructional modifications can probably help ELLs acquire literacy more effectively in English?

generally very low literacy levels that place them at ever-higher risk of school failure and limited social and economic opportunities.

In this chapter we address specifically what we know from research about promoting higher levels of literacy attainment among ELLs when they are instructed in their second language. In Chapter 5 we address second-language academic instruction in the other curricular areas.

When ELLs are in a primary-language program, as we discussed in Chapter 2, the only real difference between effective literacy instruction for them and effective instruction for non-ELLs is probably the language of instruction and language of the curriculum materials. The same principles of effective teaching and learning should generally apply. There might be differences in literacy instruction having to do with the characteristics of the primary language itself. For example, some have argued that teachers must take a more syllabic approach when teaching Spanish-speaking children to read in Spanish, due to the syllabic nature of Spanish orthography (that is, the writing system used to represent spoken words). Although there is really no hard evidence one way or the other, it is plausible that different languages might call for different instructional or curricular approaches. This is particularly likely to be true when the language is nonalphabetic, such as Chinese, where characters stand for concepts rather than sounds.

Similarly, there might be cultural differences in how speakers of non-English languages need to be instructed that go beyond simply instructing in that language. Many educators and researchers have argued that to be effective, instruction must be accommodated to the culture of the students. As we will discuss in Chapter 7, there is not a great deal of evidence to support this proposition, except in some limited ways. For the moment, therefore, let's assume that when children are in primary-language instruction, the only difference between effective instruction for them and effective instruction for English speakers is the language that is used.

However, primary-language instruction often is not possible. This can be for many reasons, from political obstacles (such as California's Proposition 227) to the absence of teachers competent in students' home language. While primary-language literacy instruction might be preferable, educators must have alternatives. And even if students' primary language is used, there will still be times when students will be learning in English, even before they have fully mastered the language. This chapter addresses the critical issue of teaching students to read in a language they are simultaneously learning to speak and understand; Chapter 5 will discuss teaching ELLs academic content more generally.

The fundamental issue in this chapter is the interplay of oral language development—being able to speak and understand a language orally—and literacy development—learning to read and write in that language. This interplay presents a huge challenge for teachers and students because each developmental process—oral language development and literacy development—is complex in and of itself, and each influences the other. With English learners, teachers have to deal with both simultaneously and in a way they do not with children who already speak English. There is of course a huge range of oral language proficiencies even among English speakers, but children who have grown up speaking English understand and speak it in a way that children who have not grown up speaking English simply do not. Thus teachers have a greater challenge in managing, promoting, encouraging, and stimulating both oral and written language development *simultaneously* for ELLs.

If this sounds complicated, that's because it is. But we will start with some comforting news: Learning to read in a second language, even if you do not know it well, is similar in many ways to learning to read in your first. Clearly, if students do not understand the language of instruction and reading materials, modifications must be made; we will discuss those in this chapter and Chapter 5. But with respect to literacy, the critical thing seems to be that ELLs need to acquire the same set of skills and concepts that students already proficient in English need to acquire to become successful readers and writers. Our job as teachers is to make sure students acquire those skills that are essential for literacy development. The best way to accomplish this goal, the Center for Research on Education, Diversity and Excellence (CREDE) report concludes, is through "focused and explicit instruction in particular skills and subskills [that will enable] ELLs . . . to become efficient and effective readers and writers" (Genesee, Lindholm-Leary, Saunders, & Christian, 2006, pp. 139–140).

We turn now to some of these literacy skills and what the research says about how to help ELLs learn and develop them.

## ENGLISH LEARNERS DEVELOPING LITERACY: KEY COMPONENTS

The report of the National Reading Panel (2000) identified several key components of literacy—phonemic awareness, phonics, reading fluency, vocabulary, and reading comprehension. The National Literacy Panel (NLP) used these as a starting point and added writing, since the charge to the NLP was *literacy* development for ELLs—not just reading—and research on English-speaking students has demonstrated the benefits of writing instruction (e.g., Hillocks, 1986). Although there are undoubtedly other important components as well, such as background knowledge, opportunities to read, and motivation, the NLP examined "the extent to which explicit teaching of these components confers a learning benefit on children who are learning English" (August & Shanahan, 2006, p. 419). Box 3.1 lists the literacy components examined by the NLP.

## Box 3.1

**Literacy Components Examined by the National Literacy Panel**

1. Phonemic awareness and phonics

2. Oral reading fluency

3. Vocabulary

4. Reading comprehension

5. Writing

The logic behind this approach makes sense. Comparable reviews for English-speaking students already existed, and a major question the NLP needed to address was whether becoming literate in English when you are learning it as a second language is similar to or different from learning to read in English when you are already fluent in the language. As the NLP put it:

> It is possible that second-language literacy development is similar for native speakers and English-language learners. If so, we would expect studies of the teaching of literacy components to be equally effective with both groups. It is also possible that linguistic context is so different for the native and second languages that English-language learners may benefit from a different regimen of instruction. (August & Shanahan, 2006, p. 419)

(The NLP also examined studies that looked at more "complex approaches" incorporating more than a single component. The NLP analyzed them separately, as will we in the next section.)

The NLP concluded that "it appears that what works with native-speaker populations *generally* works with English-language learners" (August & Shanahan, 2006, p. 437, emphasis in the original); that is, the key components identified for English speakers' literacy development are probably also key components for ELLs. But there were some important qualifications. First, the instructional benefits to ELLs were not the same for all components: Phonemic awareness and phonics, vocabulary, and writing instruction produced positive effects for ELLs; the effects of instruction in oral reading fluency and reading comprehension were at best questionable. Second, the effects of instruction on any of the components were quite variable and generally lower for ELLs than they were (based on previous reviews) for English speakers. We don't really know whether instruction in some components really is *not* effective for ELLs or if it's just that researchers have not yet identified the instructional elements that make it effective for ELLs. We return to this issue in the last part of the chapter when we discuss instructional modifications for ELLs' literacy instruction.

Nonetheless, explicit teaching of key literacy components tends to be important for all learners, and it probably is also important—perhaps especially important—for ELLs. Because English learners lack proficiency and fluency in English, instruction that is not sufficiently explicit, that is vague or indirect, is likely to be confusing or at best not very productive.

## Phonemic Awareness and Phonics

The role of phonics in reading instruction has been contentious for a very long time. Yet the evidence is very clear that phonics instruction and instruction in the related concept of "phonemic awareness" (being able to hear and manipulate the individual sounds in words) help children learn to read. These are by no means the only things teachers need to concern themselves with when students are first learning to read, but they are extremely important. And they are especially critical for children who don't readily grasp the "alphabetic principle," which is the absolutely critical understanding that letters represent sounds and that words are formed by groups of letters representing particular sounds.

The NLP reviewed five studies that showed the benefits of structured direct instruction for the development of these key early literacy skills among ELLs. A study in England, for example, found that Jolly Phonics had a stronger effect on ELLs' phonological awareness, alphabet knowledge, and their application to reading and writing than did a Big Books approach (Stuart, 1999). Another study of mostly Spanish-speaking beginning readers in the United States demonstrated the effects of a highly structured, direct instruction, phonics-oriented reading program (Reading Mastery). There were effects on word attack skills after 4–5 months of instruction; after 15 months, there were also higher scores on vocabulary and comprehension. Other studies the NLP reviewed also showed similar effects of directly teaching the sounds that make up words, how letters represent those sounds, and how letters combine to form words. In other words, even though students are learning English, they can still learn these critical skills and concepts *in English*. Studies conducted since the NLP and CREDE reports appear to continue to provide evidence of the benefits of directly teaching beginning phonological and decoding skills to English learners (e.g., Vaughn et al., 2006).

The NLP review also described a study that showed Spanish speakers could be directly taught to discriminate between English sounds that are difficult for them, such as *cheat* and *sheet*. Since there is no *sh* sound in Spanish, these students often cannot tell the difference, or pronounce differently, words such as *cheat* and *sheet, chair* and *share,* or *chuck* and *shuck.*

This study suggests that these discriminations can be directly taught. The study taught only a few sounds and did not try to gauge the impact of this discrimination training on literacy development, however, so we don't know what the effect is on learning to read and write.

The scenario in Box 3.2 illustrates a phonics lesson for English learners.

---

**Box 3.2**

**Elementary Phonics Lesson Scenario**

Mr. G. is teaching a phonics lesson on the *ea* sound to his 20 first-grade students prior to reading an anthology story about going to the beach. Most are English learners whose primary language is Spanish. They are mostly at early intermediate English proficiency levels based on the state ELD assessment.

Mr. G. shows a picture of children playing in the sand at the beach and asks them to identify the beach and the sea in the picture. He tells the students that today they are going to be learning to read words that have the long *e* sound that they hear in *beach* and *sea,* and then they are going to listen to a story about going to the beach. But first he says, "Let's review the way we learned to make the long *e* sound yesterday. Tell your partner the way we learned to spell long *e.*" Mr. G. gives the class a minute to do this while he walks around to gauge what students remember from the day before.

After partners share, Mr. G. makes a web with *ee* in the center and lines going outward, like wheel spokes. He asks students to think of words with *ee.* After giving them 15–20 seconds to think, he calls for volunteers. Students then offer *sleep, bee, keep,* etc. Mr. G. goes on: "OK, the new way to write the long *e* sound is *ea.*" Mr. G. points out that in Spanish this is the same sound that is made by the letter *i* or the word *y* (*and*).

Mr. G. has the students practice saying single syllable, medial long *e* words. He shows the students the long *e* (*eagle*) card used by the reading program the school uses and explains that they are learning words where the *ea* says long *e.* As he writes each *ea* word on the board, the students use a blending routine. S-ea...*sea,* b-ea-ch...*beach,* b-ea-d...*bead.* Mr. G. shows a picture of the sea, the beach, and a necklace bead. He models blending several words, and then the students repeat after him.

---

## Oral Reading Fluency

Reading fluently is not merely reading fast or turning the pages quickly, although skeptics like to ridicule it in this way. Reading fluently involves reading accurately and with intonation consistent with the meaning of the text, which involves reading with appropriate speed so that what is being read actually makes *sense*. The reason reading fluency is important is not complicated. Readers need to read with ease because if they are focusing too much attention on merely recognizing words, they are unable to concentrate on what matters, which is the meaning. We might admire fluent, expressive oral reading, such as in a public reading performance, and this is a good skill to have. But reading fluency—just like phonics—is really a means toward an end: comprehension. Reading too slowly or too fast can both interfere with comprehension. We know from research and experience that comprehension is enhanced when reading is fluent and compromised when it is not.

While dozens of fluency studies have been conducted with English speakers, the NLP uncovered only two with English learners. The results of these studies are not very conclusive about the role of oral-reading fluency in ELLs' English literacy achievement. In one study, fluency instruction for Spanish-speaking ELLs in Grades 2–5 led to more rapid gains in oral-reading fluency (including reading accuracy) but did not translate into improvement in comprehension. In the second study, fluency instruction in Spanish for Spanish-English bilinguals led to improvements in oral-reading fluency and in reading comprehension. However, the results were measured in Spanish reading; there was no test of impact on English reading.

## Vocabulary

Vocabulary is, of course, very important for literacy development, since it is impossible to understand fully what you read unless you understand almost all of the words. There is a long history of vocabulary research among English speakers, and the results are well established (Biemiller, 2004): Good vocabulary instruction has a strong effect on students' ability to learn words. It has a more modest, although still significant and meaningful, effect on reading comprehension. Studies of vocabulary instruction for ELLs, although far fewer, show the same thing: Students are more likely to learn words when they are directly taught, and in the case of students old enough to read, vocabulary instruction helps improve reading comprehension modestly. Just as with English speakers, ELLs learn more words when the words are embedded in meaningful contexts and students are provided with ample opportunities for their repetition and use, as opposed to looking up dictionary definitions or presenting words in single sentences.

A fifth-grade study reviewed by the NLP showed the effectiveness of vocabulary instruction that included these characteristics:

- Explicit instruction of word meanings
- Using words from texts appropriate for and likely to interest the students

- Exposure to and use of words in numerous contexts, such as the following:
  o Reading and hearing stories
  o Discussions
  o Posting target words
  o Writing words and definitions for homework

The instructional elements used in this study were comparable to vocabulary instruction that has been found to be effective for English speakers (e.g., Beck, McKeown, & Kucan, 2002). The experimental program also included elements specifically geared to English learners, such as using cognates from students' first language (Spanish); we review these elements later in the chapter when we discuss modifications for ELLs.

Two other studies reviewed by the NLP also showed that "thicker" vocabulary instruction—more activities that taught the words directly and gave students more experiences with the words in different contexts—led to better results. In one study Spanish-speaking first graders worked on words presented in meaningful narratives, dictated their own sentences using the words, and examined pictures that illustrated the words. This led to children learning twice as many words, as compared to children who were expected to learn words presented in the context of an individual sentence.

Based on these few studies, the key seems to be explicit teaching of vocabulary words using instruction that goes beyond the traditional practice of giving a definition and illustrating with a sentence. Students certainly need definitions and illustrative sentences, but they also need exposure to words in different contexts and opportunities to use them in different ways, what might be characterized as "rich" or "thick" instruction.

## Reading Comprehension

Comprehension is, of course, what reading is about. We read to comprehend; everything else is a means to this end. But even if everything else is in place—decoding skills, reading fluency, vocabulary—students can still improve their reading comprehension by using comprehension strategies. A great deal of research exists on comprehension strategies among English speakers. This research shows that teaching students strategies such as questioning themselves while reading, making predictions, summarizing, and monitoring their comprehension improves their reading comprehension. But the research is limited for ELLs. The NLP located only three such studies that explicitly included ELLs (compared to over 200 reviewed by the National Reading Panel for English speakers).

The evidence on the effectiveness of reading comprehension instruction for ELLs is quite weak. One study found no effects of training ELLs to ask themselves questions as they read. In another study, students receiving reading strategy instruction such as KWL (what I *Know*; what I *Want* to know; what I *Learned*) outperformed other groups on a comprehension measure, but the differences were not statistically significant. A third study permitted no conclusions about the effects of strategy instruction because of a serious design flaw. At the moment there is more evidence that primary-language support (as we cited in the previous chapter) improves comprehension. We think it is highly likely that we can help ELLs improve their comprehension by teaching comprehension skills directly in English (probably depending on their level of English proficiency), but readers should realize that as of yet, there is little research that actually corroborates this.

Another aspect of reading comprehension is the background knowledge that readers bring to the text. Just as comprehension is very difficult if you cannot read words accurately and fluently or don't know the meanings of almost all of the words, comprehension is also very difficult if you lack the requisite background knowledge to make sense of what you are reading. We return to this topic later in this chapter (in the "Instructional Modifications" section) and again in Chapter 7, which deals with sociocultural factors, including culturally related background knowledge.

## Writing

The final specific component addressed by the NLP was writing. Consistent with the writing research on English speakers, writing instruction helps improve ELLs' writing. One study compared the effects of structured writing (teachers assigned topics and provided feedback on content, word usage, and syntax; students were expected to correct all errors) to a free-writing condition where there was much less direction or structure by the teacher. Both groups demonstrated improvements over the six weeks of the study (subjects were low-achieving Spanish speakers in a summer program). But students in the structured-writing condition outperformed students doing the free writes. Another study, this one in Hong Kong, found that when ELLs worked on writing in peer groups, discussed their papers, and then edited them, there was greater improvement when compared to the traditional method of teacher assignments followed by paper corrections. Two other writing studies looked at the effects of peer response on ELL students' writing. One found that writing quality improved; the other did not (although the amount of writing increased).

What little writing research there is on ELLs shows that feedback, either from teachers or peers, and revision tend to improve student writing. This finding is very similar to findings with English-speaking populations: Students' writing improves when they are given specific feedback to use when revising their writing.

# ENGLISH LEARNERS DEVELOPING LITERACY: "COMPLEX APPROACHES"

In addition to studies that addressed specific literacy components such as phonics, comprehension, and writing, the NLP also reviewed studies that addressed several components simultaneously, what the NLP called "complex approaches to literacy." These included a very wide range of programs and approaches. This is such a diverse group of studies that it is nearly impossible to come to any general conclusion about what works. In addition, results were rarely straightforward in any study and would be hard to describe without going into the sort of detail that many readers will find very tedious. So at the risk of superficiality, here is a brief recounting of what most of these studies have found:

- Success for All (Slavin, Madden, Dolan, & Wasik, 1996), the most thoroughly researched whole-school reform model in the country, has demonstrated positive effects on various outcomes, including Spanish reading and English word attack skills, although the effects have not been consistent from one study to the next.
- Encouraging students to read has produced different results depending on the language in which students are encouraged to read. On the one hand, encouraging reading in the home language has not been found to affect English literacy skills; one study in fact found negative effects on reading comprehension after encouraging reading in the home language for seventh and eighth graders. This finding seems to run counter to the research discussed earlier in this chapter on the benefits of primary-language instruction; however, encouraging reading is not equivalent to providing instruction, so the two sets of results might not be comparable. In contrast to studies of reading in L1, encouraging reading in English after school hours seems to have a positive effect on English reading achievement. Three studies, each with different ELL groups in different countries—Pakistani English learners in the United Kingdom, Fijian speakers learning English (the school language), and Cantonese students learning English in Honk Kong—found comparable results.
- Tutoring and remediation studies reviewed by the NLP either did not report or did not find effects of remediation on English literacy skills (one of these found positive effects of a Spanish version of Reading Recovery on Spanish reading). However, more recent studies conducted by Sharon Vaughn and colleagues that appeared after the NLP and CREDE reports completed their work have found fairly strong effects, on both English and Spanish reading, of intensive small-group interventions for ELLs at risk for reading problems (see Vaughn et al., 2006).
- A cooperative learning study found positive effects on Spanish writing and English reading for early primary children.

- Teaching ELLs "effective use of time" seemed to enhance their reading achievement, but the study's findings are uncertain because there were differences between the groups at the beginning.
- Enriched literacy instruction that provided extended and structured opportunities for reading, writing, speaking, and listening (e.g., instructional conversations, assigned independent reading, literature logs) might promote English literacy achievement for ELLs who were transitioning from Spanish to English literacy instruction.
- A study of middle school ELLs found that English-captioned TV helped students learn academic content more effectively than either (1) reading textbooks or (2) TV without captions. However, the effects were not general for all units, and there were pretest differences between the groups.

As we can see, there is a wide range of approaches and strategies that have been tried to promote English literacy development among ELLs. Many of these—although not all—have at least some limited evidence of effectiveness. However, there are few studies, and they are scattered and diverse, so it is difficult to come up with many generalizations in which we can have confidence. This in itself is important for educators to know, since books, articles, and workshops are filled with "research-based" prescriptions for educating ELLs. One has to wonder what research these authorities are invoking. The research is, in fact, sparser than many people realize.

In our estimation, the most defensible and useful thing we can conclude from this research is that most of the strategies and approaches that help English speakers become literate also help English learners become literate. To test this proposition for themselves, readers should go back over the findings as we have reported them in this chapter and judge. Are the instructional strategies and approaches found to be helpful for English speakers also strategies and approaches applicable to ELLs? Although there are clearly some exceptions, we think the answer is generally yes: The fundamentals of effective literacy instruction apply to ELLs, just as they do to English speakers. Direct teaching of the components of literacy (e.g., phonics, vocabulary, writing) help ELLs improve their literacy skills, just as they help English speakers improve their literacy skills. And more enriched literacy learning opportunities, as represented by the "complex approaches" reported by the NLP, also promote improved literacy outcomes.

There is one important qualification: The effects of what might be called "generic" effective instruction are generally smaller for English learners than they are for English speakers; in some studies the effects of instruction were actually nil. That is, instruction in the components of literacy and instruction using a more multifaceted approach tend to get positive results, but the results are generally more modest than they are for English speakers. As we'll see in the next section, the most likely explanation for this is that English learners do not benefit from instruction in

English to the same extent that English speakers do for the simple reason that ELLs are limited in their English proficiency. As a result, ELLs probably require certain instructional modifications or adaptations for the instruction to be fully meaningful. This is the final topic we address in this chapter. They also undoubtedly need English language development instruction, which we take up in Chapter 4 and again in Chapter 5 when we discuss academic language.

# WHAT INSTRUCTIONAL MODIFICATIONS ARE NEEDED FOR ENGLISH LEARNERS LEARNING TO READ?

As we have indicated, a key finding from the NLP's review was that the impact of literacy instruction in English tends to be weaker for English learners than for English speakers. Even though what works for English speakers tends to work for English learners, it might not work as well. And there are even some aspects of literacy instruction—oral-reading fluency and reading comprehension strategies—for which we presently have little evidence that they work at all for ELLs.

Why should strategies that are successful with English speakers be less or even *not* successful with English learners? There are probably many factors. Whatever the explanation, the double challenge ELLs face is undoubtedly important: learning academic content and skills while simultaneously learning the language in which these skills are taught and must be learned. Reading comprehension requires not only reading skills—accurate and fluent word recognition, understanding how words form texts that carry meaning, and how to derive meanings from these texts—but also fundamental language proficiency—knowledge of vocabulary, syntax, and conventions of use that are the essence of "knowing" a language. Learners who know the language can concentrate on the academic content. But learners who do not know the language, or do not know it well enough, must devote part of their attention to learning and understanding the very language in which that content is taught. Teachers must always keep in mind this enormous dual challenge that ELLs face. It's a challenge that most ELLs probably have difficulty meeting without additional instructional supports.

### Phonological and Phonics Instruction Might Be an Exception

A possible exception to the NLP finding that ELLs tend to benefit less from generic instruction comes in the earliest stages of learning to read, when the focus is on sounds, letters, and how they combine to form words that can be read. Understanding the system of letters and sounds to be able to recognize (or write) words is referred to as "word-level skills." In contrast, understanding how to comprehend what you're reading or write a meaningful message requires "text-level skills," that is, many words put together that form a "text." During the earliest stages of reading development, word-level skills are particularly important, and instruction should target phonological awareness, decoding, and word recognition. The NLP found that instruction at this stage of reading development is as effective for English learners as it is for English speakers. Good, clear, systematic, focused instruction in phonological awareness and phonics seems to be effective, regardless of language proficiency. ELLs probably need even clearer and more systematic instruction than do English speakers, but this is probably a difference in degree, not a different type of instruction.

The NLP also reported that the progress made by ELLs at this early stage of learning to read is comparable, and in some cases even superior, to that of English speakers. If so, this suggests we can expect essentially identical achievement for English learners and English speakers at this early reading stage, again, assuming the instruction is clear, focused, and systematic. On the one hand, it's plausible that when language requirements are relatively low—as they are for learning phonological skills, letter-sound combinations, and decoding—ELLs can make progress that is equivalent to that of English speakers.

But on the other hand, we must be very careful, since almost all of the studies used by the NLP to support this particular conclusion were conducted with ELLs in Canada. The ELL population in Canada is very different from the ELL population in the United States. Because of highly restrictive immigration laws, and far less illegal immigration from countries with low levels of formal education, ELLs in Canada come from homes that in some cases are even more advantaged than the native-born Canadian population. Of course, there is a range of socioeconomic statuses and parent education levels among ELLs in Canada just as there is among populations everywhere. But overall, Canadian ELLs are of a much higher socioeconomic status than ELLs in the United States. As we have discussed, by far the majority of ELLs in this country are of Mexican and Central American descent; family economic and educational levels are lower than that of the U.S. native-born population and lowest of any immigrant group. The Canadian ELL population comes from families with higher income and education levels, so conclusions about Canadian ELLs cannot be directly applied to ELLs in the United States. A recent article in a leading Canadian newspaper reports higher achievement levels among Canadian immigrant children than immigrant children in other countries due, at least in part, to the fact that Canada "largely attracts educated newcomers" (Mahoney, 2007). (Interested readers should see the Immigrating to Canada Web site at http://www.cic.gc.ca/english/immigrate/index.asp.)

Regardless of whether most ELLs in the United States can actually keep pace with native English speakers in the earliest stages of learning to read, there is no question that as children advance in their literacy development and must acquire and develop text-level skills, the challenges mount. The content they read gets more challenging, language demands increase, and more and more complex vocabulary and syntax are required. The need for instructional modifications to make the material more accessible and comprehensible will almost certainly increase accordingly. Not surprisingly, ELLs' language limitations begin to impede their progress most noticeably as vocabulary and content knowledge become more relevant for continued reading (and general academic) success, around the third grade. This is also why it is critical that teachers work to develop ELLs' English oral language skills, particularly vocabulary, and their content knowledge from the time they start school, even before they have learned the reading basics.

Chapter 5 will go into more detail on possible instructional modifications (sometimes referred to as "sheltered instruction") for ELLs to help them acquire academic content. In the rest of this chapter we will discuss modifications that have shown promise for two important aspects of reading development—vocabulary and reading comprehension.

## Modifications for Vocabulary Instruction

As we have discussed, there are probably many features of effective vocabulary instruction that hold true for both English learners and English speakers. One example of such instruction is using clear, comprehensible definitions and explanations with exposure to and opportunities to use the words in different contexts and in different ways. In a study that appeared after the NLP and CREDE reports were completed, Collins (2005) found that ELL preschoolers acquired more vocabulary when teachers explained words contained in a storybook read to them. In a more recent study of science vocabulary, Spycher (2009) found that ELL and English-proficient kindergartners benefited equally from "intentional and explicit" vocabulary instruction that was part of rich science content instruction, multiple readings of narrative and expository texts, and scaffolded opportunities to engage in academic talk with the words and concepts students were learning.

But while ELLs in both studies learned vocabulary from clear and explicit explanations, just as the English speakers did, Collins (2005) also found that children who began with lower English scores learned less than did children with higher English scores. That is, knowing less English made it harder to learn additional English. What might have helped the children with lower initial English proficiency gain more English vocabulary? Another preschool study (Roberts & Neal, 2004) found that pictures helped children with low levels of oral English learn story vocabulary (e.g., *dentist, mouse, cap*). That is, the *visual representation* of concepts, not just a language-based *explanation*, provided children with additional support in learning the vocabulary words. There is scant research on this topic, but we would also expect that songs, rhymes, chants, or other additional opportunities to use and repeat words would help build vocabulary among young English learners.

What about for older children? Some clues for vocabulary instruction are offered in a study by Carlo et al. (2004), which was included in the NLP report. Carlo et al. examined the effects of a vocabulary instruction program on Spanish-speaking ELL and English-speaking fifth graders. Although the approach Carlo and colleagues took was based on principles of vocabulary instruction found to be effective for children who speak English, they included additional elements specifically for the ELLs: activities such as charades that got learners actively involved in manipulating and analyzing word meanings; writing and spelling the words numerous times; strategic uses of Spanish (e.g., presenting the words in Spanish before teaching them in English, previewing lessons using Spanish texts, providing teachers with translation equivalents of the target words, using English-Spanish cognates, such as *supermarket* and *supermercado*); and selection of texts and topics on immigration that were expected to resonate with the Mexican and Dominican immigrant students who participated in this study.

As we reported already, the experimental program produced relatively strong effects in terms of students' learning the target vocabulary and smaller, but still significant, effects on reading comprehension. Particularly noteworthy is that the effects of the program were equivalent for ELLs and English-speaking students. This demonstration that, with additional support, a program can have a similar impact on both ELLs and English speakers is very important. We cannot determine which of the extra ELL supports explains the program's impact, since they were all implemented together, but as a group they produced positive effects.

In Box 3.3, we see a variety of strategies that might aid in vocabulary instruction for ELLs.

## Modifications for Reading Comprehension

The National Reading Panel, which only reviewed research on English speakers, identified eight types of reading comprehension instruction that had positive effects; some of these effects were very strong, as much as a 35 percentile-point boost in comparison to a student who did not receive this instruction. In contrast, as we reported already, the NLP found the effects of comprehension strategy instruction on ELLs were so weak that there is a real question as to whether there was any effect at all. Reading comprehension is likely to be an area where ELLs will need considerable additional support. We have seen in this chapter how vocabulary instruction can help boost reading comprehension. In Chapter 2 we discussed several types of primary-language support that might help promote reading comprehension. These supports include previewing English reading material in the primary language, teaching metacognitive

**Box 3.3**

### Elementary Vocabulary Lesson Scenario

Mr. G. has the class gather on the rug to begin the vocabulary portion of the lesson before reading aloud a story about the beach. Mr. G. has already decided on seven vocabulary words he wants the students to know: *beach*, *castle*, *tunnel*, *sea*, *dig*, *build*, and *sand*. To tap prior knowledge and generate vocabulary, he asks the students if they have ever been to the beach and what things they might see there. If they haven't been to the beach, he asks them if they have ever seen a movie about the beach or the sea (such as *Finding Nemo* or *The Little Mermaid*). He also shows several pictures of the beach and the sea to build background knowledge.

Using the pictures and their prior knowledge as support, he writes on a chart, "Things I can see at the beach!" Students name things they might see at the beach as the teacher records the words on the chart. Next, Mr. G. does a "picture walk" with the book, asking the students what they see in the pictures; students offer new additions to the word chart. Mr. G. points out the identified target words in the pictures if the students have not offered these words. Mr. G. has also brought in a small jar of sand for the students to pass around and touch.

Mr. G. has sentence strips on the board that say, "What is this?" and "This is (a/an) _____." He asks the students to listen while he asks, "What is this?" He answers his own question, "This is sand." He then asks the students, "What is this?" He holds up his hand as a wait signal, waits two or three seconds, then signals the students to answer in unison, "This is sand." For the verbs, he asks, "What is he doing?" and models the response, "He is digging." He proceeds this way with the other target vocabulary words.

He uses cognates (along with pointing) to clarify and to help the Spanish-speaking students connect concepts they already know in Spanish to the words in English. For example, he says, "The children are building a castle, *un castillo*, and digging a tunnel, *un tunel*, in the sand." He has the students role play that they are building a castle and digging a tunnel.

He asks students, based on the pictures and the vocabulary words, to tell their partners what they think the story will be about. First Mr. G. gives some examples of using the target vocabulary in sentences. He says, "I think they will swim in the sea. I think they will build a castle in the sand."

reading strategies (such as "reciprocal teaching") in the primary language, and pointing out similarities and differences between English and the student's home language (e.g., real and false cognates).

Another instructional modification suggested by the NLP and CREDE reviews that could help ELLs' reading comprehension is the use of reading materials with familiar content (we revisit this topic in Chapter 7, "Social, Cultural, and Family Influences"). The NLP found that when ELLs read texts with more familiar material, their comprehension improves. (However, studies found that ELLs' proficiency in the language of the text influences comprehension much more than familiarity with passage content, which suggests—as one would expect—that boosting English language proficiency will help promote reading comprehension in English.) In one study reviewed by the NLP, for example, Spanish-English bilingual children and monolingual English speakers were given a test of reading comprehension and an oral test of prior knowledge to determine familiarity with the content of the reading test. For those passages where the Hispanic students' prior knowledge was equivalent to that of the English speakers, their reading comprehension was also equivalent. However, when the bilingual students' prior knowledge was less than that of the English speakers, their comprehension was also lower.

This relationship between content familiarity and text comprehension is of course not unique to any one group. In general, we all comprehend familiar material more readily. This is why having wide-ranging background knowledge is so important for reading comprehension. Success as a reader is not determined solely by reading skills such as decoding, fluency, or using reading strategies. Readers need to know content (and the vocabulary that goes with it) if they are to understand fully what they read. The importance of background knowledge for comprehension is also one of the arguments made in support of primary-language instruction to bolster students' content knowledge, as we discussed in the last chapter.

Given the formidable language challenges English learners face, teachers should be aware of how they can help students experience additional success by providing familiar reading matter. This can be accomplished in different ways. One possibility is to provide reading materials that resonate with students' experiences, as Carlo et al. (2004) did when they used texts and topics on immigration with the Mexican and Dominican immigrant students who participated in their study. Another approach is making sure students have sufficient exposure to the content in texts they are to read prior to their reading the material. For example, teachers can teach a unit in which students *learn* about a topic for several days before being expected to read and comprehend written materials about the topic. In other words, while English speakers from about middle elementary grades and up can be expected to learn by reading, English learners must be more familiar with the content they are reading if the material is to be comprehensible to them. Teachers must always keep in mind that the job of comprehension is made doubly challenging for English learners since they must comprehend content that is written in a language they are simultaneously learning.

ELLs learning to become literate in English and English speakers learning to become literate (in English) have more in common that people might realize. Both groups of students need to learn the same skills and concepts. Both benefit from explicit help and instruction in the components of literacy and from instruction that provides more enriched, complex literacy learning opportunities. ELLs clearly benefit from good instruction in some of the components of literacy (phonological and phonics skills, vocabulary, writing), while the evidence for the benefits of instruction in other components (oral-reading fluency and reading comprehension) is more tenuous. This does not mean that promoting fluency and providing comprehension instruction do not matter for ELLs. We strongly suspect they do. But the research is lacking.

We do have good evidence that more multifaceted approaches to promoting literacy development among ELLs—that is, instruction not focused on any one literacy component such as decoding or vocabulary—can also be effective. And, finally, the bulk of the research reviewed by the NLP and CREDE reports suggests that effective direct teaching and teaching using interactive approaches (such as "instructional conversations") that challenge ELLs academically make a positive contribution to their literacy growth. It is almost certain, however, that modifications are needed if we are to make English literacy instruction as effective for ELLs as it is for English speakers.

## RECOMMENDATIONS

- **The foundation of an effective English literacy program for ELLs is similar to that of an effective literacy program for English speakers—instruction in phonemic awareness, phonics, oral-reading fluency, vocabulary, reading comprehension, and writing.** In addition, students need enriched literacy instruction that targets more complex sets of skills and concepts and ample opportunities to learn content that will provide the background knowledge essential for successful reading. All of these should be part of ELLs' English literacy curriculum and instruction.

- **Use instructional modifications to help English learners acquire literacy skills in English.** Although research on these is sparse, the following are candidates for effective modifications: making instructions and expectations extremely clear, focused, and systematic; using visuals, including graphic organizers, to illustrate concepts; using the primary language for support (e.g., preview what students will read, explain skills and strategies students will use, use cognates for vocabulary instruction); use of reading matter with familiar content; and additional practice and repetition.

- **Teach ELLs literacy skills explicitly.** Students in general benefit from explicit instruction, but ELLs probably even more so since they have the double challenge of learning literacy skills while learning to speak and understand English. Vague, unclear, open-ended instruction and expectations are unlikely to serve ELLs well, particularly the more limited they are in their English proficiency.

- **In addition to explicit skills instruction, use interactive teaching with ELLs, where teachers challenge students cognitively and linguistically.** As important as direct teaching is, ELLs also need opportunities for engaging in challenging interactions; teachers must be careful to structure the interactions appropriately, depending on students' language and skill levels.

## REFERENCES

August, D., & Shanahan, T. (Eds.). (2006). *Developing literacy in second-language learners: Report of the National Literacy Panel on language-minority children and youth.* Mahwah, NJ: Lawrence Erlbaum.

Beck, I., McKeown, M., & Kucan, L. (2002). *Bringing words to life: Robust vocabulary instruction.* New York: Guilford Press.

Biemiller, A. (2004). Teaching vocabulary in the primary grades. In J. F. Baumann and E. J. Kame'enui (Eds.), *Vocabulary instruction: Research to practice* (pp. 28–40). New York: Guilford Press.

Carlo, M. S., August, D., McLaughlin, B., Snow, C. E., Dressler, C., Lippman, D. N., et al. (2004). Closing the gap: Addressing the vocabulary needs of English-language learners in bilingual and mainstream classrooms. *Reading Research Quarterly, 39,* 188–215.

Collins, M. (2005). ESL preschoolers' English vocabulary acquisition from storybook reading. *Reading Research Quarterly, 40,* 406–408.

Genesee, F., Lindholm-Leary, K., Saunders, W., & Christian, D. (2006). *Educating English language learners.* New York: Cambridge University Press.

Guthrie, J., Schafer, W., & Hutchinson, S. (1991). Relations of document literacy and prose literacy to occupational and societal characteristics of young black and white adults. *Reading Research Quarterly, 26,* 30–48.

Hillocks, G. (1986). *Research on written composition.* Urbana, IL: National Conference on Research in English.

Kaestle, C. (1991). *Literacy in the United States.* New Haven, CT: Yale University Press.

Mahoney, J. (2007, Sept. 18). Canadian immigrant students outpace counterparts elsewhere. *The Globe and Mail.* Retrieved September 21, 2007, from www.theglobeandmail.com.

Miller, G. (1988). The challenge of universal literacy. *Science, 241,* 1293–1299.

Murnane, R., & Levy, F. (1996). *Teaching the new basic skills: Principles for helping children to thrive in a changing economy.* New York: Free Press.

National Reading Panel. (2000). *Report of the National Reading Panel—Teaching children to read: An evidence-based assessment of the scientific research literature on reading and its implications for reading instruction (report of the subgroups).* Washington, DC: National Institute of Child Health and Human Development. Retrieved from http://www.nichd.nih.gov/publications/nrp/report.cfm.

Roberts, T., & Neal, H. (2004). Relationships among preschool English language learners' oral proficiency in English, instructional experience and literacy development. *Contemporary Educational Psychology, 29,* 283–311.

Slavin, R., Madden, N., Dolan, L., & Wasik, B. (1996). *Every child, every school: Success for all.* Thousand Oaks, CA: Corwin.

Spycher, P. (2009). Learning academic language through science in two linguistically diverse kindergarten classes. *The Elementary School Journal, 109,* 359–379.

Stuart, M. (1999). Getting ready for reading: Early phoneme awareness and phonics teaching improves reading and spelling in inner-city second language learners. *British Journal of Educational Psychology, 69,* 587–605.

Vaughn, S., Mathes, P., Linan-Thompson, S., Cirino, P., Carlson, C., Pollard-Durdola, S., et al. (2006). Effectiveness of an English intervention for first-grade English language learners at risk for reading problems. *The Elementary School Journal, 107,* 154–180.

# 4

## *Promoting English Oral Language Development*

Developing high levels of English oral language proficiency should be a priority for teachers of English learners. Regardless of what we think of using the first language for classroom instruction (see Chapter 2), academic success in the United States requires proficiency in oral English. Proficiency in English, according to the Center for Research on Education, Diversity and Excellence (CREDE) report,

- What is the difference between conversational and academic English?
- What do we know about effective approaches to promoting English language development (ELD) for ELLs?
- How long does it take English learners to become fluent in English?
- How should ELD instruction be organized?
- Does interaction with English speakers improve ELLs' English proficiency?

means acquiring vocabulary; gaining control over conventions of use; understanding nuances of the language; knowing how to interact successfully with others in different contexts such as informal meetings, classroom discussions, and extended conversations; listening to or telling stories; and listening to or providing explanations of academic content. The agenda is deep and wide.

Why is English oral language proficiency important? The answer to this question might appear self-evident. Yet in our experience, not everyone accepts that oral English proficiency should be a high priority. Fortunately, educators working in schools and the parents of ELLs don't need to be convinced. They know that oral English proficiency is important because English is the principal language of interpersonal communication, business, written and printed media, and academic discourse in the United States. Despite considerable historical and current language diversity in this country, many non-English-speaking enclaves, and numerous accommodations for non-English speakers—from driver's license tests to medical translators to voting ballots—the person with limited English proficiency is limited in all sorts of ways in this country. This is why so many immigrant parents place such emphasis on their children's learning English, sometimes to the point where they resist primary language (or bilingual) instruction, wrongly assuming it impedes developing English proficiency (see Chapter 2). While we believe the United States could benefit from additional linguistic diversity (as is characteristic of most countries around the world), English proficiency is essential for full participation in this society.

In school, oral English proficiency is important for at least two reasons. First, it helps promote access to the core educational curriculum we want all students to learn in *all* content areas—math, science, history, social studies, reading, and language arts, as well as art, music, physical education, and any other subject matter a school or district determines is part of the curriculum for all students. Since native language programs are not the norm in the United States (see Chapter 1), and are even more rare as students progress through the grades, students who are limited in their English cannot rely on primary language programs to provide access to the core curriculum. Nor can ELLs always count on instruction that takes into account their limited English while still providing access to the core curriculum (as described in Chapters 3 and 5). Even with such instruction, students might be hampered or slowed down since the teacher has to tailor instruction to language proficiency levels. Students who lack English proficiency will thus always risk being at a disadvantage, compared to their English-proficient peers, in learning academic content.

The second reason English oral proficiency is important is that it almost certainly contributes to English literacy development. It should be no surprise that English *oral* proficiency is correlated with English *literacy* (reading and writing) skills. The CREDE and National Literacy Panel (NLP) reports agree on this: When students have higher levels of oral language proficiency (e.g., vocabulary, syntax, ability to relate narratives and provide explanations), they also tend to have higher reading levels. While we must be careful about interpreting correlations as indicating cause and effect (see Chapter 1), it is reasonable to suppose that better command of oral English will contribute to improved reading and writing ability.

Surprisingly, neither report directly addresses the question of whether oral English proficiency is correlated with general academic success in English. Based on the correlation between oral proficiency and literacy achievement, however, we would expect students with higher levels of oral

English proficiency also to have higher levels of achievement in content areas. The CREDE report did find that students who are proficient in *both* English and their home language outperform students who are monolingual only in English, but it discusses no direct links between English proficiency and ELLs' academic achievement, citing an absence of research.

## A SURPRISING LACK OF RESEARCH

In general this is an aspect of the ELL literature with a surprising absence of research. Most surprising is how little research there is examining the effects of different approaches to oral English language development. The CREDE review (the only one of the two reports that directly addressed English language development) uncovered only *one published study* that evaluated "the effects of instruction and training on oral language outcomes" (Genesee, Lindholm-Leary, Saunders, & Christian, 2006, p. 21) for ELLs. The study (by Michael O'Malley and colleagues) found that adolescent ELLs' oral language development was aided when they were taught to use certain strategies such as note taking, selective attention, and summarizing as they listened to lectures. The CREDE report, reasonably, concludes that ELLs' oral language development might be enhanced if they are explicitly taught and trained how to apply these strategies. But the research base is too thin to permit great confidence in this conclusion.

The CREDE report says that "there is virtually no U.S. research on how classroom instruction might best promote more academic aspects of oral language development" (Genesee et al., 2006, p. 19). Although this is changing, educators still do not have an adequate research base to answer many important questions, particularly about promoting *academic* language proficiency, a topic we turn to next. Many educators believe they are using research-based practices to address academic language needs when, in fact, they are relying on theoretical orientations or plausible-sounding approaches (Coleman, 2006). Many readers will be surprised to learn that research has not shown any superiority of one approach over another to ELD for ELLs or to helping ELLs gain increasing access to grade-level curriculum. Consequently, educators should be skeptical—and ask lots of questions, such as *"Where is the evidence?"*—when brochures, staff developers, or advocates make claims about the effectiveness of particular programs.

## ACADEMIC AND CONVERSATIONAL ENGLISH HAVE DIFFERENT CHARACTERISTICS

Despite the surprising absence of research, there are still some important lessons to be learned from existing research. One is that when it comes to school, "oral English fluency" refers not just to conversational fluency but to fluency with *academic* language as well.[1] Full English proficiency for English learners includes more than mere fluency in conversation. It also means knowing English well enough to be academically competitive with native-English-speaking peers (Hakuta, Butler, & Witt, 2000). The distinction between academic and conversational proficiency was first articulated by Jim Cummins (1979, 1981), who coined the terms *basic interpersonal communicative skills* (BICS) and *cognitive academic language proficiency* (CALP) 30 years ago and has written extensively about them in many publications since (e.g., Cummins, 1989, 2000). The concepts have had an important impact on the field, but the terms *BICS* and *CALP* are used less frequently than they were 10–20 years ago and have been subject to critiques by analysts pointing out their various "boundaries and limitations" (Baker, 2006, p. 175). Nonetheless, the distinction between relatively informal, less demanding *conversational* language and the more formal, generally more demanding *academic* language necessary for school success continues to inform our thinking and planning for the education of ELLs. This has been particularly true in the past decade when standards and accountability requirements have gotten increasingly demanding for all students, including ELLs. (See Chapter 5, "Academic Instruction in a Second Language," for more on academic language in the context of instruction in academic content areas.)

What this means for teachers is that they must be mindful that academic language is distinct in important respects from conversational language and tends to make different cognitive demands on listeners and speakers. Academic language is what is used in textbooks, lectures, and discussions about academic content. The language is more abstract, deals with concepts (e.g., multiplication, democracy, organisms) rather than more immediate or concrete topics, and tends to be more complex than conversational language. Readers and listeners must understand it, often with minimal context, when reading a book or listening to someone deliver a lecture.

It is possible, however, to overdraw the distinction between conversational and academic language and make it too categorical (Baker, 2006; Valdés, 2004). As with all generalizations, we must be cautious because there are exceptions. Some conversations can be cognitively challenging and require information that not everyone has. Moreover, there are plenty of examples of situations where the language appears to be a hybrid on the "conversational-academic continuum" rather than neatly falling into *either* the conversational or academic category. For example, talking about a movie's theme, setting, or the motivations of its central characters, or describing the

---

[1]Our thanks to Guadalupe Valdés for her feedback and suggestions on the academic-language portions of this and the following chapter. All errors of fact and interpretation, of course, remain our own.

strategy behind intentionally walking a batter in baseball can take place in informal conversational contexts but requires the use of relatively more abstract, decontexualized language. Table 4.1 compares conversational and academic language, and a hybrid of the two, along several dimensions of language features and use. The critical point for teachers to keep in mind is that they *cannot* approach ELD instruction merely from the standpoint of promoting children's conversational and interpersonal skills in English, as useful and important as they are.

One indication that conversational and academic languages are distinct comes from correlations between oral English proficiency and English reading achievement. When a measure emphasizes conversational language (sometimes called "everyday"; see column 1 of Table 4.1), the correlation with reading achievement is relatively low. However, when a measure emphasizes academic language (e.g., content-oriented and more abstract; see the righthand column of Table 4.1), the correlation with reading achievement is relatively high (Genesee et al., 2006; see "Oral Language" chapter by Saunders and O'Brien). For example, correlations between reading achievement and the Basic Inventory of Natural Language, which emphasizes everyday language, are lower than correlations between reading achievement and the Woodcock Language Proficiency Battery (WLPB), which is very academically oriented. These findings suggest that conversational fluency has less bearing on reading development compared to academic language skills. Teachers must be mindful of this important distinction and not make judgments about academic language skills based on their assessment of conversational language skills. Nor can they assume that developing students' conversational skills will by itself adequately promote academic language skills.

This is really where the challenge lies—helping ELLs develop oral (and written) language skills that will make them *academically* competitive. The CREDE report says researchers and educators have found that most ELLs can achieve conversational fluency relatively easily within one, two, or maybe three years. But academic language fluency is a bigger challenge and takes longer to develop. This is where considerable effort, energy, and resourcefulness must be expended, by both researchers and educators. We discuss academic language in more depth in Chapter 5's focus on academic instruction.

## APPROACHES TO PROMOTING ENGLISH LANGUAGE DEVELOPMENT

Over the years, numerous approaches have been used to help students develop English language skills or, more generally, learn a second language. In practice, most programs use elements of many approaches and methods, so it would be misleading to draw too hard a line among them.

**Table 4.1** The Continuum of Conversational to Academic Language

| | Conversational Language Tends to . . . | "Hybrid" Area | Academic Language Tends to . . . |
|---|---|---|---|
| Shared background knowledge | • Be embedded in meaningful contexts, drawing upon shared background knowledge, or existent in the moment of the conversation. When people converse, they are often talking about a specific topic about which they both have at least some direct knowledge, experience, and relevant information. | While discussing unfamiliar content in either a conversational or academic context, adequate background knowledge is purposefully provided by a speaker. Oral and written language may make ample use of visuals such as charts, posters, photos, and the like to make academic content more highly contextualized for the reader or listener. | • Be relatively decontextualized, relying largely on information contained in the language of the oral or written text; the reader or listener has to provide her own relevant background knowledge or context necessary for understanding. |
| Nonlinguistic aides to understanding | • Be fundamentally interpersonal. Face-to-face exchanges allow for contextual and interpersonal cues such as gestures, facial expressions, and intonation. | In academic contexts, speakers use interpersonal cues such as gestures, speaking rate, pauses, and intonation to make relatively abstract messages more comprehensible. | • Be fundamentally impersonal. Emphasis, mood, and tone must be communicated primarily through words and content. There is no, or very limited, face-to-face exchange. |
| Vocabulary | • Use more familiar everyday words. Precise meanings are generally not as important as maintaining conversational flow and arriving at an adequate mutual understanding. | In conversational contexts, speakers use unfamiliar words and expressions (e.g., *parameters*) so that relatively simple concepts might be more difficult to understand. | • Use specific and less familiar vocabulary that can be technical, abstract, and carry precise meanings the listener or reader is expected to understand. |

| | Conversational Language Tends to . . . | "Hybrid" Area | Academic Language Tends to . . . |
|---|---|---|---|
| Grammatical shortcuts | • Frequently use grammatical shortcuts, such as *and* or pronouns whose meanings are apparent to the participants in the context of the conversation. Talk can include nonstandard, colloquial speech. | Speakers and writers can make academic content more accessible by using a conversational tone, which can include figures of speech, familiar expressions, and less density of ideas. | • Frequently use specific grammatical, organizational, and presentation elements. Writing and speech is more formalized and structured. Tone is set by an impersonal, declarative style to establish authority. Language is denser, with more ideas presented. |
| Language to express cognitive functions | • Place fewer explicit cognitive demands on the reader or listener; events and persons are known, familiar, and concrete; inferences, analyses, and presentations of reasoned arguments are typically less prominent. | Everyday conversational events can be cognitively complex and challenging, such as retelling a TV episode logically and showing a causal sequence or a child presenting an argument for why he should be able to stay out late without parents' direct supervision. | • Be used for more complex cognitive functions, such as summarizing, analyzing, and explaining; relating what is read to other ideas; evaluating and critiquing arguments; composing reasoned, well-developed texts; interpreting and solving word problems. |
| Examples | Husband and wife exchange information about what they did at work that day; each is generally familiar with what the other one does and his/her work colleagues. | An individual trying to follow a conversation about unfamiliar persons and complicated events is provided background information or shown pictures. | Reading a book or listening to a lecture on recent advances in genetics.<br><br>An encyclopeda article on the Electoral College. |

*(Continued)*

**Table 4.1** (Continued)

| Conversational Language Tends to . . . | "Hybrid" Area | Academic Language Tends to . . . |
|---|---|---|
| An animated conversation between friends discussing a date the night before. | Conversation with someone who speaks with little expression, uses little eye contact, and does not respond to others' behaviors or responses. | A professor of contemporary literature presents a postmodern poststructuralist analysis of *The Sound and the Fury*. |
| Two experienced divers, planning a scuba diving trip, decide locations and gear they will need. | A speaker uses expressions such as "if you juxtapose the two" instead of "if you put them side by side" or asks, "What are the parameters here?" instead of "What do we need to consider?" | A sociologist is interviewed on a news program and asked to explain the impact of the economic downturn on community-based organizations. |
| Softball players arguing over whether a player was out when she ran to first base. | A person explains to her friend what it was about a television program that she found so moving and insightful. | A student must explain his reasoning, in writing, when solving a mathematical word problem. |
| Ordering from a menu at a family restaurant. | | Coworkers at a public relations firm must present and argue for their proposed campaign to rehabilitate the tarnished image of a client. |
| Friends watching a movie and making occasional comments, observations, and jokes to each other. | | |
| Taking turns during show-and-tell sharing with the class a favorite toy from home. | | |

(left margin label: Examples)

*Source:* Categories based on Fillmore and Snow, 2002; Scarcella, 2003; Schleppegrell, 2001; Valdés, 2004.

Nonetheless, it is useful to keep in mind some of the most important approaches to second-language learning, which include the following (see Brown, 2007, for more detailed information; see also Krashen & Terrell, 1983, for another perspective).

*Grammar translation* is the classical approach to second-language teaching. The focus is on making learners proficient in understanding the second language through translation and study of the language's formal grammar. Students are presented with lists of vocabulary and grammatical rules in the second language that they then use to translate written texts from one language to the other. There is relatively little emphasis on the spoken language, although this method also uses isolated practice, drills, and oral grammatical exercises. There is also very little focus on communicative ability.

The *audio-lingual method*, first popularized in the 1950s, stresses oral production of correct speech in the second language. It is an example of a "behaviorist" approach in that the emphasis is on what learners say—that is, their *verbal behavior*—rather than on what they are thinking or how they mentally organize knowledge and skills about the second language. Audio-lingual methods use listening to examples of correct speech in the target language followed by student repetition—sometimes a great deal of repetition. Aspects of this method can still be found in many popular programs designed to teach a second language. The emphasis is on repetition and practice of vocabulary, phrases, and the various sentence forms used in a language. Aspects of the behavioral approach are receiving renewed attention through the use of direct instruction (described later in this chapter), with its emphasis on the importance of practice to gain fluency.

The *natural approach* (see Krashen & Terrell, 1983) emphasizes communication and conversation with very little, if any, attention to grammatical analysis or repetition outside of a meaningful context. This approach is based on the assumption that we learn a second language in much the same way we learn a first language—in meaningful situations where the focus is on *using* the language for genuine communication. The basis of this approach is that learners will naturally—that is, without direct teaching, practice, or drills—acquire a second language if provided the right context and input. Learners use "comprehensible input" and natural communicative strategies (e.g., pointing and other bodily actions that clarify the words being spoken) to make sense of and learn to speak a second language. Individuals, in other words, learn a language not by studying it or being taught directly but through meaningful interactions with others.

*Direct instruction* aims to teach students well-defined and targeted skills as efficiently and directly as possible. Direct instruction is not specific to second-language learning; various forms of direct instruction have been used in numerous curricular areas, most notably reading and mathematics (for reading, see Carnine & Silbert, 1979). Direct instruction also includes having students use and practice aspects of the language they are learning; in other words, they practice producing what one researcher has called "comprehensible *output*" (Swain, 1985). In principle, any aspect of language—vocabulary, verb forms, grammar, idiomatic expressions, conversational conventions—can be targeted for explicit teaching. Key features of this approach include clear identification of concepts and skills to be taught, an instructional sequence that targets all learning needs, explicit instruction aimed at mastery of identified concepts and skills, instructional feedback to correct errors and misconceptions, sufficient opportunity for practice and review, and application of acquired language skills in meaningful contexts. Current proponents of direct instruction in second-language learning argue that direct teaching and frequent exposure and practice, embedded in meaningful contexts, are the keys to second-language acquisition (Dutro & Moran, 2001).

Despite the many theories and approaches to second-language learning for ELLs, as the CREDE review found, we know remarkably little about their relative effectiveness. We believe that direct, or explicit, teaching methods should be given serious consideration, primarily because of how critical *academic* language proficiency is (explained more fully later in this chapter). We cannot discard completely nor embrace fully any one single approach to second-language learning. It is highly likely that different approaches, for example, explicit teaching or interactive discussions or simulations, work for different instructional purposes and, in fact, can complement each other.

Around the time the CREDE report was completed, several publications appeared (Ellis, 2005; Lyster, 2007; Norris & Ortega, 2006) that supported this perspective: Effective second-language instruction provides a combination of (a) explicit teaching that helps students directly and efficiently learn features of the second language such as syntax, vocabulary, pronunciation, and norms of social usage and (b) ample opportunities to use the second language in meaningful and motivating situations. We do not know whether there is an optimal balance. But there is every reason to believe that successful second-language instruction comprises elements of both types of learning opportunities for second-language learners.

## HOW LONG DOES IT TAKE ENGLISH LEARNERS TO BECOME FLUENT IN ENGLISH?

There has been considerable discussion over the past 30 years regarding how long it takes non-English speakers to become fully fluent in English. Advocates of simply immersing students in English point to how quickly children appear to acquire a second language and wonder what all the fuss is about. In contrast, advocates of using the primary language for instruction (as discussed in Chapter 2) say it's not so simple. Children might acquire *conversational* aspects of a second language rapidly, but this is misleading.

As we have discussed, it's *academic* language that will most heavily influence academic opportunities and school success. Here, the process of developing full English proficiency is longer and more difficult, particularly when a child is in a home environment that is not rich with the sort of language most supportive of developing academic language skills in *any* language (see Hart & Risley, 1995). The real question is this: How long does it take ELLs to become sufficiently fluent in academic English so that they can meaningfully and productively participate in mainstream English instruction? The question is especially critical if students are not in a solid primary-language program that will assure adequate academic progress as they acquire English language skills.

Our ability to answer this question is hampered by inadequate research and the absence of a uniform or generally accepted sequence of "levels" of second-language proficiency. Different researchers, professional organizations, and states have different schemes. Box 4.1 presents descriptions of one plausible sequence of language-development levels, from beginning to advanced English speaker.

A handful of studies have reported data on the oral English proficiency development of ELLs. Using a creative and insightful synthesizing approach, the CREDE report came to the following conclusions about these studies:

1. ELLs required four to six years to attain what could be considered "early advanced" proficiency, or a 4 on a 5-point scale such as the one shown in Box 4.1. We can thus expect that if an ELL begins school in kindergarten, advanced oral proficiency skills are likely to emerge sometime between the third and fifth grades, although it can vary enormously for different children.

2. Average oral English proficiency began to *approach* (not even necessarily attain) native-like proficiency (a Level 5) in Grade 5 in fewer than half of the studies.

3. Students moved relatively rapidly from beginning to intermediate levels (from 1 to 3), but progress was slower between Level 3 and advanced Levels 4 and 5. Students could be around a Level 4 in Grade 3 but then take two years to move close to a Level 5 (but note this was a level attained in fewer than half the studies, as indicated above).

4. Despite year-to-year progress, the gap between ELLs and native speakers widened by the fifth grade. This was particularly evident in the one study that specifically addressed rates of oral language proficiency attainment using the WLPB. As we have discussed, the WLPB is the most academically oriented of the language proficiency measures used.

5. The CREDE report says that these observed patterns were similar, regardless of whether children were in all-English programs or programs making extensive use of the primary language.

**Box 4.1**

## Levels of Language Development

Although simplifications of a complex phenomenon, proficiency levels can be briefly and generally described as follows:

*Beginning* (Level 1): At first there might be no verbal response (sometimes referred to as "preproduction" or "silent period"), but later, students respond in single words and two-word phrases. Students can repeat words and short phrases and answer simple "who, what, when, where" and yes-or-no questions requiring one- or two-word responses. They can understand and follow a few simple commands and participate in telling a story using isolated words after listening to a story prompt.

*Early Intermediate* (2): Students hear and repeat beginning, middle, and end speech sounds. They use routine expressions, common vocabulary, and can respond using phrases and simple sentences. They can ask and answer simple questions, describe a picture prompt using common vocabulary, understand and follow simple commands, and tell a story using incomplete sentences and fragments after listening to a prompt.

*Intermediate* (3): Students respond in longer sentences and with more detail. There is more experimentation with sentence variety. They know a variety of verb forms and tell a story with some complete sentences after listening to a story prompt. These students can follow simple instructions in an academic context and participate (although haltingly) in simple academic discussions if the vocabulary is controlled and supports are provided (illustrations, demonstrations, gestures, and other redundant information to aid comprehension).

*Early Advanced* (4): Students respond with detail and a more extensive vocabulary in more complex sentences. They can sustain a conversation. Early advanced students understand implied meaning and use standard grammar with fewer errors than before. They can tell a story in a logical sequence using details and basic sentence construction after listening to a story prompt. These students can follow more difficult directions in an academic context and participate more fully in academic discussions, even when provided with fewer supports.

*Advanced* (5): Students initiate and negotiate appropriate discourse, using varied grammatical structures and vocabulary. They comprehend multiple meanings and figurative and idiomatic language. Advanced students can follow complex instructions in an academic context and tell a story using fluent sentences and details after listening to a story prompt. Their proficiency is near native-like, and they face few, if any, linguistic obstacles to full academic participation.

*Source:* Adapted from California Department of Education (2008) and Krashen & Terrell (1983).

# A NEED TO FOCUS ON
# ACADEMIC ENGLISH PROFICIENCY

There are two important points to make about these conclusions: First, as advocates of primary-language instruction have argued (Chapter 2), most ELLs take years to develop the level of English proficiency—*academic* English proficiency—required for full participation in all-English classrooms. It does not take much imagination to conclude that if (a) students are functioning at less than high levels of English proficiency and (b) instruction is only offered in mainstream academic English, these students will not have access to the core academic curriculum. They will have virtually no chance of performing at a level remotely similar to that of their English-speaking peers. This is one of the strongest rationales offered for providing academic instruction in the primary language: Students will fall behind in their academic progress if they are only instructed in English, but their English skills are inadequate for full-on academic instruction.

Second, we do not really know why acquiring academic English proficiency seems to take several years, which is more than most people assume children need to become fluent speakers of a second language. One possibility is that this long period—five to seven or more years—is inherent in learning a second language to a sufficient degree that one can compete academically with students who are already proficient. Another possibility is that most ELLs in the United States come from home backgrounds where there is less academic language in *any* language—not just in English (see Chapter 7, where we discuss home and family factors). A third possibility is that there might be a general lack of emphasis on academic-language instruction in school. Educators might assume that given a language-rich environment, where there is an abundance of text, environmental print, and oral and written language opportunities, students will "naturally" acquire high levels of academic oral English proficiency. This lack of emphasis might be responsible for students' simply moving along, year to year, making what progress they can without benefit of explicitly articulated programs designed to maximize their academic English acquisition.

We do not have the research to evaluate these alternative explanations for why English language development is slower than most people assume it is—or ought to be. Each might provide a part of the explanation. However, since we are particularly interested in what educators can do to accomplish important educational goals, we recommend paying particular attention to the third explanation. A language-rich environment is in itself probably not sufficient for optimal academic language development for ELLs. A language-rich school environment is certainly desirable but we suspect not enough to accelerate English language development adequately. Instead, educators probably must be more directive, structuring explicit language learning opportunities to develop vocabulary, syntax, and other aspects of how the English language functions, combined with ample opportunities (at school and home) for practice and meaningful use of the language.

Studies reviewed in Chapter 3 suggested that, at least in the short run, explicit teaching can help ELLs acquire vocabulary, which is of course an important part of language development. A recently published study also suggests that a comprehensive and structured approach to teaching language directly and explicitly can help accelerate young children's English language development. Tong, Lara-Alecio, Irby, Mathes, and Kwok (2008) found that providing kindergarten and first-grade students with an "English-oracy intervention" resulted in accelerated ELD growth (as measured by tests of vocabulary and listening comprehension). The ELD intervention, which was equally effective with students in either English immersion or bilingual education, comprised (a) daily tutorials with a published ELD program, (b) storytelling and retelling with authentic, culturally relevant literature and leveled questions from easy to difficult, and (c) an academic oral language activity using a "question of the day." Students who received the experimental treatment received more ELD instruction than students in the control schools (75–90 minutes per day for the experimental vs. 45 minutes per day for the controls); moreover, the students with lowest levels of English proficiency received 10–20 minutes of additional instruction provided by trained paraprofessionals. It is impossible to rule out the effects of additional time, independent of the particular curriculum and instruction used. Nonetheless, the study is important in demonstrating the possibility of accelerating English language development, at least in the early grades, through intensive, organized instruction.

## HOW SHOULD ENGLISH LEARNERS BE GROUPED FOR ELD INSTRUCTION?

Educators often ask how ELLs should be grouped for instruction. Should they be grouped with other ELLs or kept with English speakers? If grouped with other ELLs, should they be with others at similar language levels or should they be in mixed-ability language groups? If grouped with others at similar language levels, for what purposes and for how much of the school day? Many studies have examined the pros and cons of different types of ability-grouping arrangements in areas of the curriculum such as reading and mathematics (Slavin, 1987, 1989). But no such research exists about grouping English learners to promote English language development.

Research on ability grouping (Slavin, 1987, 1989) suggests the following:

1. Keeping students of different achievement or ability levels in entirely separate ("homogeneous") classes for the entire school day (and throughout the school year) leads to depressed achievement among lower-achieving students with little to no benefit for average and higher-achieving students. A possible exception is for extremely high-achieving students (sometimes referred to as "gifted"), whose achievement can be significantly enhanced in homogeneous classes with other extremely high-achieving students.

2. Students in mixed ("heterogeneous") classrooms can be productively grouped by achievement level for instruction in specific subjects (e.g., math or reading). Grouping can be done with students in the same classroom or students in different classrooms (the latter is sometimes called a "Joplin plan"). In contrast to keeping students in homogeneous classes throughout the day (#1, above), grouping students by achievement in specific subjects will result in enhanced achievement at all ability levels provided (a) instruction is well tailored to students' instructional level and (b) students are frequently assessed and regrouped as needed to maintain an optimal match with their instructional needs; that is, students are taught what they need to know to make continuous progress.

To what extent do these findings apply to English language development for ELLs? There are many ways that second-language learning might be very different from learning traditional school subject matter. Consequently, it's difficult to know if we can apply findings based on research in reading and mathematics to English language development. On the other hand, and to the extent that second-language learning is analogous to learning in any other curriculum area, findings from the ability grouping literature serve as a useful starting place to make decisions about how to group ELLs.

These findings suggest that ELLs should not be segregated into all-ELL classrooms, much less into classrooms consisting of all high-achieving ELLs or all low-achieving ELLs. Instead, ELLs should be in mixed-ability (heterogeneous) classrooms but then grouped by English language proficiency specifically for ELD instruction. Moreover, they should be regularly assessed to monitor their progress and make certain that instruction and group placement are well suited to their language learning needs (but note that ELD assessments to inform instruction leave much to be desired; see Part V in the NLP report, "Student Assessment"). Presumably, as ELLs gain in English language proficiency, they can and should receive increasing amounts of their instruction with students who are already proficient in English.

## INTERACTIONS WITH ENGLISH SPEAKERS

One aspect of the grouping issue has to do with whether ELLs will use and practice English more if they have more opportunities to interact with fluent English speakers and, in addition, whether these opportunities to use more English will then help promote English proficiency. As the CREDE report says:

> Most programs for ELLs incorporate some provision for the integration or mixing of ELLs and native or fluent English speakers. . . . The assumption is that such integration . . . provides ELLs with worthwhile language learning opportunities. (Genesee et al., 2006, p. 28)

Common sense suggests that mixing ELLs and English speakers should help promote ELLs' language development. But the research findings suggest a slightly more complicated scenario. Some studies have found a positive correlation between English language use and English language development, but once again keep in mind that correlation should not be equated with causation. Increased English oral interaction might be the result, not the cause, of improved English proficiency. The CREDE report concludes that increasing opportunities for oral English use among ELLs and having those opportunities translate into improved English language development "involves more than simply pairing ELLs with native or fluent English speakers" (Genesee et al., 2006, p. 28). Several aspects contribute to a surprisingly complex set of factors.

First, students' language choices when interacting with other students in the class are influenced by the instructional language used in the classroom. The CREDE report found that ELLs are more likely to interact with peers in English in classes where English is the language of instruction; when Spanish is the language of instruction, ELLs choose to interact more in Spanish. This means that when students are in programs that use substantial amounts of primary language, teachers probably have to take additional steps to encourage ELLs to engage in English language interactions with their peers (when assignments or activities call for interactions in English).

Second, even when interacting with other students in English, these interactions don't necessarily lead to productive English learning opportunities for ELLs. Students might be interested in completing tasks rather than in promoting language learning. The CREDE report cites a study in a sixth-grade classroom where the native English speakers typically cut short their interactions with ELL students in their cooperative groups. One

English speaker was quoted as saying, "Just write that down. Who cares? Let's finish up." There was little in the interactions that could be expected to promote academic language learning among the ELLs.

Third, beginning ELLs are probably less likely to benefit from interactions with English speakers than are more advanced ELLs. Beginning ELLs lack the language skills to communicate productively with English speakers about academic tasks. In addition, as illustrated above, English speakers might lack the skills (and possibly the motivation) to interact with their beginning-ELL peers in ways that will enhance their language skills.

Fourth, interactions between ELLs and English speakers might actually decrease over the course of the school year. Only one study reported this finding, so we do not know how general it is nor why it might happen. One (admittedly speculative) possibility is that perhaps neither ELLs nor English speakers find their academic interactions to be particularly productive or satisfying, so they taper off over the year. This possibility is suggested by a study reviewed by the NLP, which found that Hispanic ELLs in cooperative groups were less effective than English speakers in obtaining help from their peers. They spoke with their heads down and did not focus their requests on specific persons, which resulted in less successful requests for help during cooperative group work.

A possible solution suggested by some studies in the CREDE report is training to help English speakers interact more productively with ELLs. In one study, pairs of ELLs and English speakers were trained using a program ("Inter-Ethnolinguistic Peer Tutoring") to promote more extensive interactions between students. The report provides few details about the content of the training, but presumably students were trained to listen and respond to each other and ask and answer questions using more elaborate responses than they normally use. The study found that ELLs who received the training (with their English-speaking peers) improved their vocabulary scores, although the improvement was not reflected in a general measure of language proficiency (the Language Assessment Scales).

The larger point is that although interactions with English speakers are probably helpful for promoting English language development among ELLs, teachers should be mindful of factors influencing ELLs' use of English with peers. Teachers need to make sure students focus on extended and productive interactions (rather than quick task completion), which might require that both ELLs and English speakers learn strategies for successful verbal interactions. Teachers should teach and model interaction strategies such as directing requests to specific individuals; providing clear, complete, and comprehensible answers; and demonstrating helpful attitudes among all participants. Teachers should also make sure that ELLs have the necessary English language skills to interact successfully with English speakers on specific academic topics and tasks.

# SHOULD ELD BE TAUGHT SEPARATELY OR INTEGRATED WITH OTHER ACADEMIC INSTRUCTION?

The final question we address in this chapter is how ELD instruction should fit into the school day: Should it be targeted at specific times, in the same way reading and math instruction typically takes place at specific times of the day? Or should ELD be combined with academic instruction integrated throughout the day in other content areas such as math, reading, science, or social studies? One could make a case for either scenario. Following is an excerpt from a lesson that is designed to specifically address ELD during a designated period of the day. Although embedded in a meaningful context, the goal of the lesson is developing language rather than learning content. In the next chapter, on academic language, we will look at a lesson that develops language by integrating a language objective into content instruction.

---

**Box 4.2**

### Middle School English Language Development Scenario

Ms. R. uses her middle school's character education program to provide the content for her fourth-period ELD class comprising intermediate and early advanced English speakers. As part of the character education program, students talk about pictures showing problematic situations that might occur with peers in school and then offer alternative solutions to solve problems. Ms. R. uses this as an opportunity to teach students the subjunctive in English (e.g., "If I were ...") and to use phrases containing the modal verbs *could* and *would*.

Ms. R. has the students sitting in tables of four to five students. She shows a large poster-size picture with students apparently excluding a single student from their group. The group seems to be talking about the student sitting alone at another lunch table. The single student looks sad. Most, but not all, in the larger group are laughing.

The teacher asks the open-ended question, "What do you see in the picture? What is the problem?" She directs the students to talk at their tables while she circulates and listens in on the conversations. She calls on volunteers to report aloud and says they should respond in complete sentences such as "We see ..." or "We think the problem is ...." Students can be creative in their responses so long as they use complete sentences and what they say is consistent with what is in the picture. This part of the lesson does not challenge students' level of proficiency, so no further instruction is needed.

The teacher then says, "Now we're going to talk about problems and solutions." She draws two boxes with an arrow leading from the first box to the second box. The first box is labeled "The Problem." Ms. R. records some of the responses offered by the students in the first box.

The second box is labeled "Possible Solutions." The teacher asks, "What is a good solution? What *could* the boy do?" She defines *could* as what is *possible* to do, not necessarily what they will do. Underneath the second box, she writes, "The girl(s) could _____." Ms. R. models, "The girl in the group who is not laughing could get up and sit with the lonely girl." The students again discuss in their groups, but this time they are all to report aloud using the word *could* in their response: "We think/agree the girl(s) could _____."

Then Ms. R. asks the students to choose the best solution from the ones offered and say what they *would* do if they were in that situation. She defines "I would" sentences as what you would *probably* do *if* you were in that situation. She points out the difference between what you *would* do and what you *will* do. She asks "What would you do?" She writes on the board and models, "If I were the _____, I would _____." She tells the class, "Usually you hear people say, 'If I *was* the boy' or 'If I *was* the girl.' But that's not how we say it in English. We say, 'If I *were*.' She tells the class she is going to call on a few people to answer the question, "What would you do if you were the _____," and she wants them to answer by saying, "If I were the _____, I would . . . ." She calls on several students, one of whom still needs a little help (which Ms. R. provides).

Once she is reasonably confident that the students understand how to use this construction, she goes on: "So talk at your table about which one your table thinks is the best solution. And I want you to use the phrase 'If I *were* _____, I would _____' and tell your group why you would do that. Then we'll share with the class." The students again discuss in their groups and then report aloud using the sentence "If I were _____, I would _____ because _____" in their responses.

---

*Note:* An upper-elementary version of this lesson can be found in the English language development scenario in Chapter 8.

---

The CREDE report did not address this particular issue because there was no research available at the time the report was written. However, a recent study found that kindergarten ELLs' English language development was slightly higher in situations where children received a separate ELD period rather than when their ELD instruction was integrated into language arts (Saunders, Foorman, & Carlson, 2006). The study was limited to kindergarten, and the effect was small (although statistically reliable), but it did show that students with the separate ELD period performed better in English oral proficiency on the WLPB than children whose ELD instruction was integrated into language arts. We should be cautious about drawing conclusions from this one limited study. But if these findings can be generalized, the cumulative effect of a separate block of ELD instruction over many years could be substantial.

This study should not be interpreted to mean that a separate block for ELD instruction should necessarily be *in place of* integrating ELD into language arts or any other subject matter instruction throughout the day. Rather, in addition to a separate ELD block focusing on language development, instruction at other times of the day, specifically designed to provide access to the core curriculum, is probably also helpful (Lyster, 2007).

## RECOMMENDATIONS

- **Make ELD instruction a priority from the moment students walk into school**, regardless of whether students are in primary-language or English-only programs. However, educators must take care that ELD not displace instruction in academic content.
- **Provide daily oral English language instruction,** perhaps 45 minutes per day. However, we lack the research to make firm, data-based guidelines.
- **Explicitly teach ELLs elements of English** (e.g., vocabulary, syntax, conventions), social conventions (e.g., greetings, conversational conventions), and strategies for how to learn the language (e.g., note taking, selective attention, summarizing).
- **Provide ELLs with ample opportunities for authentic and functional English use.** Learning the elements of a language is very useful, but without extensive use (comprehending and producing the language), it is probably impossible to acquire high levels of proficiency.
- **Continue ELD instruction *at least* until students reach Level 4 (early advanced)** and possibly through Level 5 (advanced or native-like proficiency). Intermediate English proficiency (Level 3) is almost certainly inadequate for success in a mainstream English classroom, starting in middle elementary school.
- **Emphasize academic language—not only conversational language.** Academic language is critical for academic success. ELD instruction should help provide the language needed for learning content in math, language arts, social studies, science, and all other curricular areas. Ideally, ELD and content area instruction will be well articulated so that students have an opportunity to apply the language they learn to their academic tasks.
- **When teaching academic language, do not focus only on vocabulary; focus on syntax and text structures as well.** For example, students need to understand how to construct a sentence or paragraph (orally and in writing) that expresses compare and contrast or cause and effect. Academic language and curriculum content are closely intertwined.

- **Group ELLs carefully**. Although ELLs should *not* be in classrooms segregated by language proficiency levels, grouping by language proficiency *specifically* during ELD instruction is likely to be effective as long as instruction is carefully tailored to students' language learning needs.
- **Structure tasks and prepare students for interactions with English speakers** so that students focus on productive verbal exchanges rather than simply finishing tasks. Teach and model strategies for successful interactions between ELLs and English speakers. Be sure ELLs have the language skills to interact productively with English speakers on academic tasks. This means that cooperative group work should provide opportunities for structured practice, not just spontaneous conversation. In primary-language programs, where students might be more likely to use primary language with peers, structure some tasks to encourage peer interactions in English.
- **Use a separate time block for ELD instruction**. A separate ELD block that targets *language acquisition* appears to be somewhat more effective than relying exclusively on integrating ELD with other parts of the curriculum. However, integration throughout the day might be used *in addition* to a separate ELD block; there is no reason to believe they are mutually exclusive. Integrating ELD is probably useful in preparing students for comprehension of their core lesson content but might be less productive than stand-alone ELD instruction for second-language learning per se. This recommendation is based on research with young children. A separate ELD period might also be beneficial for secondary students, whether as a separate class or a time set aside within the content class. However, we know of no research that examines student outcomes and addresses the benefits of a separate ELD time for middle and high school students.

# REFERENCES

Baker, C. (2006). *Foundations of bilingual education and bilingualism* (4th ed.). Clevedon, UK: Multilingual Matters.

Brown, D. (2007). *Principles of language learning and teaching* (5th ed.). White Plains, New York: Pearson.

California Department of Education. (2008). *California English language development test (CELDT): Reporting and using individual 2008–09 results.* Sacramento, CA: Author. http://www.cde.ca.gov/ta/tg/el/resources.asp.

Carnine, D., & Silbert, J. (1979). *Direct instruction in reading.* Columbus, OH: Merrill.

Coleman, R. (2006). *The role of school districts in the selection and support of English language development programs and approaches.* Unpublished doctoral dissertation, University of Southern California, Los Angeles.

Cummins, J. (1979). Cognitive/academic language proficiency, linguistic interdependence, the optimum age question and some other matters. *Working Papers on Bilingualism, 19,* 121–129.

Cummins, J. (1981). Age on arrival and immigrant second language learning in Canada. A reassessment. *Applied Linguistics, 2,* 132–149.

Cummins, J. (1989). *Empowering minority students.* Sacramento, CA: California Association for Bilingual Education.

Cummins, J. (2000). Putting language proficiency in its place: Responding to critiques of the conversational/academic language distinction. In J. Cenoz & U. Jessner (Eds.), *English in Europe: The acquisition of a third language* (pp. 54–83). Clevedon, UK: Multilingual Matters.

Dutro, S., & Moran, C. (2001). Rethinking English language instruction: An architectural approach. In G. García (Ed.), *Reaching the highest level of English literacy* (pp. 227–258). Newark, DE: International Reading Association.

Ellis, R. (2005). Principles of instructed language learning. *System, 33,* 209–224. www.sciencedirect.com.

Fillmore, L. W., & Snow, C. (2002). What teachers need to know about language. In C. Adger, C. Snow, & D. Christian (Eds.), *What teachers need to know about language* (pp. 7–53). McHenry, IL: Center for Applied Linguistics and Delta Systems.

Genesee, F., Lindholm-Leary, K., Saunders, W., & Christian, D. (2006). *Educating English language learners.* New York: Cambridge University Press.

Hakuta, K., Butler, Y. G., & Witt, D. (2000). *How long does it take English learners to attain proficiency?* Linguistic Minority Research Institute. (ERIC Document Reproduction Service No. FL026180). Retrieved from http://www.lmri.ucsb.edu/publications/00_/hakuta.pdf.

Hart, B., & Risley, T. R. (1995). *Meaningful differences in everyday experiences of young American children.* Baltimore: Paul H. Brookes.

Krashen, S., & Terrell, T. (1983). *The natural approach: Language acquisition in the classroom.* Hayward, CA: Alemany.

Lyster, R. (2007). *Learning and teaching languages through content: A counterbalanced approach.* Philadelphia: John Benjamins.

Norris, J., & Ortega, L. (2006). *Synthesizing research on language learning and teaching.* Philadelphia: John Benjamins.

Saunders, W., Foorman, B., & Carlson, C. (2006). Do we need a separate block of time for oral English language development in programs for English learners? *Elementary School Journal, 107,* 181–198.

Scarcella, R. (2003). *Accelerating academic English: A focus on English language learners.* Oakland, CA: Regents of the University of California.

Schleppegrell, M. J. (2001). Linguistic features of the language of schooling. *Linguistics and Education, 12*(4), 431–459.

Slavin, R. (1987). Ability grouping and student achievement in elementary schools: A best-evidence synthesis. *Review of Educational Research, 57,* 293–336.

Slavin, R. (Ed.). (1989). *School and classroom organization.* Hillsdale, NJ: Lawrence Erlbaum.

Swain, M. (1985). Communicative competence: Some roles of comprehensible input and comprehensible output in its development. In S. Gass & C. Madden (Eds.), *Input in second language acquisition* (pp. 235–253). Rowley, MA: Newbury House.

Tong, F., Lara-Alecio, R., Irby, B., Mathes, P., Kwok, O. (2008). Accelerating early academic oral English development in transitional bilingual and structured English immersion programs. *American Educational Research Journal, 45,* 1011–1044.

Valdés, G. (2004). Between support and marginalisation: The development of academic language in linguistic minority children. *Bilingual Education and Bilingualism, 7,* 102–132.

# 5

## *Academic Instruction in a Second Language*

This chapter is closely related to Chapter 3 in that it deals with instructing students in academic areas in a language they are simultaneously learning, and to Chapter 4 in that a core issue is the development of academic language—the language needed for academic success. It differs from the preceding chapter, how-

- What do we mean by academic instruction?
- What are the similarities and differences between "generic" effective instruction and "sheltered" instruction?
- What is the role of academic language in academic instruction?
- What can we say from research on effective academic instruction in the content areas for ELLs?

ever, in that it is not primarily about English language development per se, although it is likely that academic instruction can be delivered in such a way that it simultaneously promotes English language development.

There are two important ways in which this chapter contrasts with Chapter 3. First, Chapter 3 specifically deals with teaching literacy, whereas this chapter addresses teaching academic content such as math, social studies, and science. Second, the research base from which we can draw in this chapter is far more limited than that which is available for literacy instruction. This is, in a sense, ironic, since "academic instruction in the content areas" would seem to include a lot more; we would expect at least as much, if not more, research to be available. But the preponderance of research conducted with ELLs has concerned literacy, primarily reading. In fact, the National Literacy Panel (NLP) report was exclusively about literacy and did not even address content area instruction. The Center for Research on Education, Diversity and Excellence (CREDE) report did address content instruction, so it will be our primary source in this chapter.

As is true for literacy, effective academic instruction for ELLs in all-English classrooms probably shares many characteristics of effective instruction with English speakers. But effective instruction for ELLs is also very likely to require additional strategies, techniques, or approaches. The question is, "What else is needed?" What modifications, adjustments, or supports (we use the terms interchangeably) do ELLs require so that they can have access to grade-level-appropriate academic content? This issue is not even close to being adequately addressed by research, yet it is one of the most pressing that teachers face. This puts a huge burden on teachers since they are required to provide meaningful and comprehensible instruction to ELLs while being equipped with less than a fully adequate and validated set of tools.

Regardless, our working assumption is that it is our responsibility— the schools' and those of us trying to support what schools do—to make classroom instruction productive for all students. As the Supreme Court said in the landmark *Lau* decision, knowledge of English can *not* be set as a prerequisite for meaningful participation in the classroom. "Imposition of such a requirement," the Supreme Court ruled,

> is to make a mockery of public education. We know that those who do not understand English are certain to find their classroom experiences wholly incomprehensible and in no way meaningful.

Thus, as is true for literacy, the challenge teachers face when providing content area instruction *in* English to students who are simultaneously *learning* English is to make the instruction comprehensible and meaningful. Anything less is, simply, unconstitutional.

In a very real sense, all students—including native English speakers— can be considered language learners. Students continually learn vocabulary, syntax, and modes of expression that expand their language capabilities as well as their content knowledge. But English learners generally lack many of the rudiments that native English speakers take for granted, rudiments that begin to build up during the preschool years before learning academic content is even an issue. English learners in an English instructional environment, in contrast, are put in the position where they are expected to learn academic content without benefit of five, six, or more years of knowledge and experience with the language. This is the challenge they and their teachers face.

# KEY CONCEPTS

This chapter addresses two topics: academic instruction and academic language. The two cannot be separated. As Schleppegrell and Achugar (2003) observe, "Even when teachers base their instruction on content area goals, they still need strategies for dealing with language itself, as content is not separate from the language through which it is presented" (p. 21). Students must not only be able to comprehend the content they are to learn, they also need academic language to express what they know in order to participate in discussions, complete assignments, and perform well on assessments.

There are several key concepts involved in this challenge, so we begin with some definitions.

## Academic Instruction

*Academic instruction* is most often thought of as content area instruction in subjects such as social studies and science. Reading instruction is also academic instruction, but because of the centrality of reading to the curriculum and to overall student success, we dealt with reading (or literacy more generally) in a separate chapter. Adequate academic instruction is, of course, important for academic achievement. Lindholm-Leary and Borsato, writing in the CREDE volume, define academic achievement as "the communicative (oral, reading, writing), mathematical, science, social science and thinking skills and competencies that enable a student to succeed in school and society" (Genesee, Lindholm-Leary, Saunders, & Christian, 2006, p. 176). Academic success requires content knowledge, use of higher-order thinking skills, and mastery of basic academic skills. Effective academic instruction is critical for all three. (See Box 5.1 for elements of effective instruction.)

---

**Box 5.1**

### Some Elements of Effective Instruction

- Clear goals and learning objectives
- Meaningful, challenging, and motivating contexts
- Connecting new learning to previous learning and background knowledge
- Clear presentation of new information
- Clear directions and explanations
- Effective modeling of new skills and procedures
- Well-organized, coherent, content-rich curriculum
- Well-designed, clearly structured, and appropriately paced instruction

*(Continued)*

(Continued)

- Active engagement and participation by students
- Opportunities to practice, apply, and transfer new learning
- Opportunities to deepen understanding of new learning
- Feedback on correct and incorrect responses
- Periodic review and practice
- Frequent formative assessments, with reteaching as needed
- Opportunities to interact with teacher and other students about the new learning

## Sheltered Instruction

Academic instruction for ELLs requires that teachers know and use strategies to make content comprehensible and accessible to students who are not fluent in the language of instruction. This set of strategies is often referred to as *sheltered instruction* or, in California, Specially Designed Academic Instruction in English (SDAIE, pronounced *suh-DIE*). (See Box 5.2 for a list of sheltered strategies.) Sheltered instruction differs from an approach developed years ago known as content-based English as a second language (ESL) instruction (sometimes called content-based English language development, or ELD). In sheltered instruction, content is determined by grade-level content standards in curriculum areas such as science and social studies. Teachers using sheltered strategies provide modifications or adjustments (through instruction and materials) to make the grade-level content accessible for ELLs. For example, seventh graders receiving sheltered history instruction are to learn seventh-grade-level history; the instruction is "sheltered" or "specially designed" so that the content becomes accessible for students who are less than proficient in English, but the content itself (concepts, facts) is at the seventh-grade level. (See Table 5.1 comparing content-based ELD to sheltered instruction.)

### Box 5.2

### Sheltered Strategies in English

- Targeting both content and English language objectives in every lesson, the latter to promote English language development explicitly and directly
- Addressing all proficiency levels whether teaching content or language objectives and focusing on higher-order cognitive skills at all levels of proficiency
- Using graphic organizers (tables, charts, semantic maps) that make content and the relationships among concepts and different lesson elements explicit

- Presenting redundant key information visually, such as with pictures, objects, and physical gestures related to lesson content
- Identifying, highlighting, and clarifying difficult words and passages within texts to facilitate comprehension and more generally greatly emphasizing vocabulary development
- Helping students consolidate text knowledge by having the teacher, other students, and ELLs themselves summarize and paraphrase
- Giving students extra practice in reading words, sentences, and stories to build automaticity and fluency
- Providing additional time and opportunities for practice, either during the school day, after school, or for homework
- Stressing highly engaging extended interactions with teacher and peers
- Offering frequent structured and unstructured opportunities for student-to-student talk in both heterogeneous and homogeneous groupings
- In interactions with the teacher, providing frequent opportunities for student talk, which encourage elaborated responses, both open-ended and those that encourage use of specific and increasingly complex linguistic features
- Adjusting instruction and speech in general (vocabulary, rate, sentence complexity, and expectations for student language production) according to students' oral English proficiency
- Using familiar content and explicitly linking new learning to student background knowledge and experience
- Employing predictable and consistent classroom management routines, aided by diagrams, lists, and easy-to-read schedules on the board or on charts, to which the teacher refers frequently

See Chapter 2 for sheltered strategies that involve use of the first language.

Although a sheltered approach differs significantly from content-based ELD, some districts use the terms interchangeably. This is a serious misconception. Content-based ELD is primarily about learning English. In content-based ELD, content areas such as social studies or science provide the topic, but the content is secondary to the English language development. Instruction will not constitute in-depth coverage of the significant concepts, skills, and information addressed in grade-level-appropriate content standards.

In this chapter we are specifically talking about teaching academic content as defined by state- or district-level content standards, not as incidental topics in ELD lessons.

## Academic Language (see also Chapter 4)

Academic instruction also requires knowledge of how academic language use differs from everyday language. Academic English refers to the

| Table 5.1 | Content-Based ELD Versus Sheltered Instruction |

You walk into a classroom and see a fourth-grade teacher teaching a lesson on the Westward Movement. She displays pictures of pioneers. On the board are the vocabulary words *pioneer, wagon, oxen,* and *prairie.* Students practice reading and reciting sentences such as the following: *The pioneers are in the wagon. The wagon is pulled by oxen. They are crossing the prairie.*

Is this a content-based ELD lesson or a sheltered-instruction history lesson? While the two may look alike to the observer, the planning for and focus of each is decidedly different.

|  | *Content-Based ELD* | *Sheltered Instruction* |
|---|---|---|
| The goal | Language development | Content instruction |
| The standards | ELD/language arts standards | Content standards (science, social studies, literature, math) |
| Teaching block | Designated ELD time | Throughout the day, all content instruction (science, social studies, literature, math) |
| How content is selected | Depth of content is determined by language objective and proficiency level.<br><br>Content may or may not correlate to the content standards for that grade level, especially if drawn from a specific ELD program.<br><br>**ELD Standard: Students exhibit early intermediate listening and speaking skills.**<br><br>1. Read simple vocabulary, phrases, and sentences independently.<br><br>2. Ask and answer questions by using phrases or simple sentences. | Depth of content based on higher-level thinking of the standard, i.e., students are asked to analyze, compare and contrast, conclude, and explain multiple causes and effects.<br><br>**History-Social Science Standard 4.3 (California Department of Education, 2000): Students explain the economic, social, and political life in California from the establishment of the Bear Flag Republic through the Mexican-American War, the Gold Rush, and the granting of statehood.**<br><br>1. Identify the locations of Mexican settlements in California and those of other settlements, including Fort Ross and Sutter's Fort.<br><br>2. Compare how and why people traveled to California and the routes they traveled (e.g., James Beckwourth, John Bidwell, John C. Fremont, Pio Pico). |

| | | 3. Analyze the effects of the Gold Rush on settlements, daily life, politics, and the physical environment (e.g., using biographies of John Sutter, Mariano Guadalupe Vallejo, Louise Clapp). |
|---|---|---|
| How language is selected | Language skills taught are determined by assessment of language needs, based on proficiency level of ELLs. It may follow a scope and sequence of language skills, depending on program and approach used. | Academic language objective involves vocabulary and syntactical structures determined by content and text structure, such as writing and speaking descriptive paragraphs, compare-and-contrast sentences, cause-and-effect sentences; asking interrogative questions for an interview; or retelling events in sequence. It may then be adjusted for different proficiency levels. |
| What is assessed? | Primarily language | Primarily content |

sort of language competence required for students to gain access to content taught in English and, more generally, that is needed for success in school and any career where mastering large and complex bodies of information and concepts is needed. As discussed in Chapter 4, academic language is different from everyday speech and conversation, what Cummins (1979) first referred to as *basic interpersonal communicative skills* (BICS). BICS are used for communicating in everyday social interactions. In contrast, *cognitive academic language proficiency* (CALP) refers to the oral and written language related to literacy and academic achievement (Cummins, 1989).

Although the terms *BICS* and *CALPS* have their limitations (see Baker, 2006), they identify a useful distinction between (a) language that is relatively informal, contextualized, cognitively less demanding, used in most social interactions, and generally learned more easily and (b) language that is more formal, abstract, used in academic and explicit teaching and learning situations, more demanding cognitively, and more challenging to learn (Bailey, 2007). The latter is the language associated with schools, texts, and formal writing (Fillmore & Snow, 2002; Scarcella, 2003). While full language proficiency is the ability to use language for a wide range of purposes, school success is particularly dependent upon academic language proficiency and fluency.

Consider the language challenges identified by one teacher in the following excerpts on manifest destiny from a fifth-grade history/social science text. Aside from their bald message of U.S. expansionism, it is striking how they illustrate the complexity of syntax and vocabulary English learners will encounter in academic texts. These two examples of academic text are each followed by an analysis of the academic language that might require explicit instruction for ELLs:[1]

> *Ex. 1:* At first the Cherokee hoped to live peacefully with settlers. They had assimilated to, or adopted, American ways of life. Some sent their children to American schools to learn to read and write English. Although they had assimilated to American ways of life, the Cherokee wanted to preserve their own language and culture (Porter, 2007, p. 528).

| Academic Language Elements Requiring Explicit Instruction | Examples |
|---|---|
| Time markers (often prepositional phrases) signal words that mark time. | • "At first" implies that later things will change. We will see a contrast.<br>• "Although" indicates a contrast between a distinct point in time and a general disposition. |
| Subject-specific vocabulary | Cherokee, assimilated, culture |
| Concept development/background knowledge | • American ways of life<br>• "Their" (Cherokee) culture<br>• American schools (schools for Native Americans had a different meaning than typical American schools) |
| Multiple word meanings and usage | adopted, preserve |
| Pronoun referents | • "Their own language and culture"<br>• "They had assimilated" |
| Nominalization (a verb or a modifier converted into a noun phrase) | • "American ways of life." |

> *Ex. 2:* During the 1840s, much of the Pacific Northwest was claimed by both the United States and Britain. Settlers moving to Oregon from the United States felt that they had the right to the land. At the time, many people in the United States believed in the idea of Manifest Destiny. They thought the United States was meant to stretch from the Atlantic Ocean to the Pacific Ocean (Porter, 2007, p. 559).

---

[1]Analysis adapted from University of California, Berkeley History Social Science Project (2009).

| Academic Language Elements Requiring Explicit Instruction | Examples |
|---|---|
| Time markers (often prepositional phrases) | "During the 1840s" doesn't mean it happened *in* 1840, rather that it spanned the decade. |
| Subject-specific vocabulary | manifest, destiny |
| Concept development/background knowledge | Pacific Northwest |
| Multiple word meanings and usage | claimed, stretch from, meant to, felt, had a right to |
| Pronoun referents | "They had the right" |
| Nominalization (a verb or a modifier converted into a noun phrase) | "Settlers moving to Oregon" |

These challenges are not unique to this textbook and are in fact quite typical of academic texts in any subject from the earliest grade levels. Certainly, to discuss each and every academic English element contained in texts students read would be unrealistic. Moreover, we really do not know which ones are the most critical to teach. But teachers do need to be aware of the complexities academic texts present to ELLs and strategically try to select key elements that might require explicit instruction or meaningful discussion.

## WHAT DO WE KNOW ABOUT EFFECTIVE CONTENT AREA ACADEMIC INSTRUCTION FOR ELLs?

Providing an all-English (or fundamentally all-English) academic program for ELLs is challenging because of the need to balance content instruction with ELD, with the added complexity that students will be at different language proficiency levels and, possibly, come from different language and cultural backgrounds. In addition, as important as English language development undoubtedly is, ELLs' academic program cannot consist of ELD, instruction exclusively; if it does, students will fall progressively further behind in their academic learning. So the challenge for teachers is to use strategies, approaches, and techniques that promote grade-level content learning (e.g., social studies, science) *and* English language development, both of which are needed for students to enter the educational mainstream (Lyster, 2007).

This is a worthy goal to which we fully subscribe. But the truth is that we lack a research base demonstrating how or even whether this can be accomplished in an all-English instructional context. As we discussed in Chapter 2, some studies have concluded that grade-level academic achievement (or close to it) and English language proficiency are more likely if students are in programs that make substantial (and, perhaps, long-term) use of the primary language. But, as we also discussed, there are methodological issues with the long-term studies that require us to interpret findings cautiously. Similarly, in Chapter 3 we reported that the NLP concluded that at the early stages of reading, ELLs can make progress that is comparable to English speakers if they receive solid systematic instruction. But limitations in those studies' applicability to the U.S. context also suggest caution. In any event, comparable progress at the early reading stages is far different from comparable progress at more advanced levels of learning that require increased proficiency in academic language.

The challenge is particularly complex in the United States because, as we have indicated, the preponderance of ELLs in this country come from homes and communities with low income and education levels, and they attend school with large numbers of children with similar backgrounds. Socioeconomic status is heavily implicated in the achievement of ELLs in the United States, in contrast to Canada, for example, where many ELLs who are the children of immigrants, or who are immigrants themselves, come from far more advantaged homes and achieve at far higher levels.

## TECHNIQUES FOR TEACHING ACADEMIC CONTENT TO ELLs

The CREDE report reviewed several studies in which educators had developed a variety of techniques for different learning styles, learning goals, and student proficiency levels (e.g., Berman, Minicucci, McLaughlin, Nelson, & Woodworth, 1995; Echevarría, Short, & Powers, 2006; Montecel & Cortez, 2002). But we don't really know which techniques are effective in producing the sort of high-level outcomes we all want (Genesee et al., 2006). The CREDE report uncovered only a handful of empirical studies that examined instructional approaches or strategies for teaching content, including one report on schools with exemplary programs in math and science. In a book that is nearly 250 pages long, the report devotes less than three pages to discussing instructional issues—as opposed to *language of instruction*—in promoting academic achievement for ELLs. The chapter on academic achievement reflects the near absence of research on this topic and is mostly devoted to comparing some form of bilingual education to all-English instruction.

The studies of academic instruction in English reviewed by the CREDE report suggest the same conclusion, although with a much smaller research base, that we reached in Chapter 3 with regard to literacy instruction: Much of what we know about effective instruction for English speakers is also applicable to English learners. The CREDE report concludes that good instruction is associated with higher student outcomes, promoting positive interactions and high-quality exchanges between teachers and students is important, and cooperative learning promotes academic engagement and improved learning. These are all aspects of effective practices for *all* learners.

So, then, what do we know about effective instructional practices for ELLs that goes beyond what we know about effective practices *in general*? Perhaps the most important conclusion one can reach is how little we can say with confidence. The CREDE report is very clear on this point:

> There is a dearth of empirical research on instructional strategies or approaches to teaching content [for ELLs]. . . . Which techniques are effective in producing high-level academic outcomes with ELLs is still an open question, as little empirical work has been done on this question. (Genesee et al., 2006, p. 190)

The most prominent instructional model to have appeared in the past few years is the Sheltered Instruction Observation Protocol, otherwise known as SIOP (Echevarría, Vogt, & Short, 2008). The CREDE report uses the SIOP as an example of an approach that targets both language and content objectives. This double-barreled approach is probably extremely important since, as we have pointed out repeatedly, the huge challenge faced by ELLs and their teachers is that they must make progress in both English language development and academic content knowledge simultaneously. It makes great sense, therefore, to make every lesson both a language and content lesson. In addition to emphasizing clearly defined content and language objectives for each lesson, the SIOP has also synthesized a large number of modifications intended to make the instructional content accessible and meaningful to ELLs and integrate them into a coherent design for planning, delivering, and assessing instruction. To date, however, one published study has examined the effects of the SIOP on student learning, and its results were very modest. Echevarría, Short, and Powers (2006) found a slight improvement in the quality of writing produced by middle-school ELLs whose teachers had received the SIOP training, compared with students of similar backgrounds (students were mostly of low socioeconomic status; more than 50 percent were Spanish speaking, but numerous other language and ethnic backgrounds were represented).

# THE DEVELOPMENT OF ACADEMIC LANGUAGE

Becoming proficient in a second language—particularly its academic aspects—is a challenge that is at least as formidable as mastering the subject matter knowledge and skills students are expected to learn as they proceed through the grades. The common misperception that the English skills required for school success will be picked up quickly by most students simply by immersing them in English is just that—a misperception (Hakuta, Butler, & Witt, 2000). In fact, as we stated in Chapter 4, the evidence reviewed by the CREDE report suggests that becoming academically proficient in English might take five or more years—not one or two. The fundamental question is whether English learners can simultaneously learn academic content and develop academic-language proficiency in such a way that they can stay on par with their English-speaking peers. We have no firm answer at the moment.

The importance of academic language to the school success of English learners is generally acknowledged, and educators are paying increased attention to it (e.g., Droga & Humphrey, 2005; Dutro & Moran, 2001; Scarcella, 2003; Schleppegrell, 2001; Zwiers, 2008). What makes academic language so challenging yet so essential for school success? As we've discussed, students usually do not have an interacting author and audience in texts they are expected to read for school. They do not have the benefit of facial expressions, tone, inflections, or gestures. Students can only rely on words on the page to understand meanings that, in face-to-face interactions, could be conveyed through various nonverbal means. Students must therefore acquire the sort of language skills that allow them to understand, talk, and write about abstract and cognitively challenging concepts that make up the core of academic learning (see, e.g., history text excerpts cited earlier). No matter how good their technical reading (decoding) and writing skills, or how good their ability to converse with others about everyday topics, students who do not have the academic language skills to comprehend and be able to speak and write about curriculum content in math, social studies, science, and the language arts will be at a serious disadvantage throughout their school careers. They almost certainly will have limited options once they leave school. As the CREDE report says, "Success in school in the long run ultimately depends critically on students' ability to read about or express abstract, complex ideas without the benefit of past experience or concurrent contextual cues" (Genesee et al., 2006, p. 67).

The relationship between academic language and content is probably reciprocal. That is, they complement each other and together contribute to a student's academic achievement (Lyster, 2007). Unfortunately, there is little if any research we can use to guide practice and policy in this regard. Krashen (2003) has argued for the importance of sheltered instruction for making content accessible to English learners, and indeed we have viable models that have translated the concept of sheltered instruction into workable schemes for planning and carrying out instruction (Echevarría et al., 2008). However, sheltered instruction does not define precisely which vocabulary and language skills to develop, how to plan a particular instructional sequence, or what aspects of language and academic content are most critical for teachers and students to focus on.

Academic language is more than content, or "technical," vocabulary. Since the studies published in the CREDE and NLP reports, some promising approaches have been used in many school districts. Michael Halliday's (1994) theory of systemic functional linguistics has received considerable attention as a way of understanding the *language* demands of academic writing and discourse (e.g., Droga & Humphrey, 2005; Schleppegrell & Achugar, 2003). According to systemic functional linguistics, the purpose of a text is what most influences syntax and word choices (Dutro & Moran, 2001; Schleppegrell, 2001). For example, to retell an event in narrative form requires knowledge of story structure and the ability to use past tense verbs and time sequence transition words. School-based texts also use organization and presentation strategies that are highly formalized and conventionalized, since the common purpose of most school-based language tasks is to present (presumably) objective information authoritatively in a highly structured fashion (Schleppegrell, 2001). Although it is certainly plausible that students must understand those aspects of academic language that are used in school and vital for understanding readings, lessons, and classroom discussions, we do not yet have data to support the idea that systematically teaching these linguistic features helps ELLs learn both academic content and academic language.

Following are portions of two lessons, one for elementary school (Box 5.3) and one for high school (Box 5.4), that illustrate sheltered instruction that also teaches academic language. The sheltered strategies include teaching content vocabulary, syntax, and language structures as they relate to the lesson's content.

## Box 5.3

### Elementary School Academic Instruction Scenario

Mrs. V. has been teaching a third-grade standards-based science unit on environments and adaptations using the saguaro cactus as a topic. The third-grade standard for life sciences is that students will understand the concept that "adaptations in physical structure or behavior may improve an organism's chance for survival." Students should know, for example, about diverse forms of life, their different structures, the different environments they live in, and how different environments increase or decrease the chances some plants and animals will survive and others will not. ELD levels in this class range from intermediate to fluent English. Mrs. V. says, "Today we are going to learn about the saguaro cactus and the ways it is adapted to its environment, that is, the reasons why it is able to survive in the desert while other plants could not."

*(Continued)*

(Continued)

She begins by asking the students what they already know about the desert and records these answers on the board. She shows a map where deserts are found and teaches the students a chant about the deserts of the world, pointing to the map as each desert is named in the chant. Mrs. V. defines a desert as a place with limited rainfall. She says not many plants can live in the desert, and if they do, they have to adapt. She writes the words *adapt* and *adaptation* on the board and introduces the word *adaptation* by showing a picture of a hare whose fur blends in to its surroundings. She states, "This hare's coloring allows it to adapt to its environment by hiding it from predators." She shows five more animal and plant pictures and asks students what the adaptation is that allows the living thing to survive in its environment. Mrs. V. then directs her students to tell their neighbors in their own words what an adaptation is.

To introduce the vocabulary and strengthen their understanding of the concept of adaptation, she draws a large outline of the saguaro cactus on the board. Mrs. V. draws in long, shallow roots and explains how these soak up surface water from rain before it dries up. She draws in pleats on the skin and explains how these pleats expand to hold more water. She demonstrates the word *pleats* by folding a piece of paper accordion style. Next she labels *waxy skin*, which holds in the water, and *spines*, which protect and shade the cactus. As she introduces each word, she adds to the drawing. After adding several more adaptations to the drawing, Mrs. V. directs the students to tell their neighbors two adaptations they learned about today.

Next, Mrs. V. draws a graphic organizer on the board to show multiple causes leading to one effect. On the left side are three vertical boxes labeled *causes*, each with an arrow leading to the box on the right, labeled *effect*. Inside the effect box, she writes, "The saguaro can live in the desert." She models on the board how she fills in one cause using the drawing she just made. She chooses "shallow roots soak up rain water" to record in one of the cause boxes. She writes this in one of the three vertical boxes. The students each have a similar graphic organizer to fill in using the other information from the drawing.

Underneath the graphic organizer are two sentences: "Because of _____, the saguaro can live in the desert" and "As a result of _____, the saguaro can live in the desert." Mrs. V. models several examples such as "As a result of shallow roots that soak up rain water, the saguaro can live in the desert." She asks for several volunteers to also suggest some possible sentences. With a choice of sentence frames and the abundance of information on the chart, the students can create a variety of sentences. The students pair up again and practice making up sentences using the information from their graphic organizer. Mrs. V. walks around the room listening to the students and checking for understanding. She tells the class they are going to write on paper these same sentences that tell about the adaptations that allow the saguaro to live in the desert.

Our thanks to Rebecca Valbuena for this lesson.

## Box 5.4

### High School Academic Instruction Scenario

Following the direct instruction portion of a lesson on sensation and perception, Mr. P. has his high school students "preread" the chapter they are about to read. In table groups he has students discuss each of the photos, illustrations, charts, and graphs. He points out the focus question at the beginning of the chapter: What is the difference between sensation and perception? He points out each subheading and, based on the titles and photos, asks students to predict what they will learn about in each section. Students then read the subheadings under the section of the chapter titled "Vision" with a partner.

One student reads a subheading section, and the partner summarizes what he just heard. They alternate until the "Vision" pages are read. Students have a note-taking graphic organizer in the form of a flow chart to record what they learned so far about vision. Each box of the flow chart is numbered to indicate a step in the process. A list of previously learned sequence words is posted. Students are asked to label each box with the appropriate sequence word such as *first, next, later, eventually,* and *finally.* Students record the process from sensory stimulus to visual perception. Each student completes his or her flow chart individually while working with a partner. Each student fills in a chart using words and pictures that tell how we sense with our eyes and perceive with our brains.

Students are first asked to share the process of sensation and perception with their partner. Volunteers are then called upon to describe the process of how they see using the words and pictures on the graphic organizer. Students are required to use the new vocabulary words (*sense* or *sensation; perceive* or *perception*) in the flow chart. The definition of *sensation* is to be in the opening sentence and *perception* in the closing sentence.

Academic language development does not take place naturally. Rather, it must be taught. While most children are familiar, albeit unconsciously, with the interactional features of oral language, for many children the features of school-based texts are much less familiar (Schleppegrell, 2001) and need to be directly taught. This is consistent with the findings in the CREDE report, which concluded that interactive learning environments that provide carefully planned direct instruction of target language skills are likely to be most effective. Language skills that are linked to literacy and academic domains should be the target of such instruction. Genesee et al. (2006) conclude from their review that "focused and explicit instruction in skills" is needed if ELLs are to become effective readers and writers (pp. 139–140).

Conversational and academic languages are not completely separate language domains (see Table 4.1). Using students' everyday experiences can help them learn academic language. The ability to adopt the appropriate language for school-based tasks can transfer from experience with the same task in a familiar context where the social purpose is apparent. So, for example, a student might know how to retell what happened on a favorite TV show or present an argument for why he should be able to go out and play basketball at the park. Students who understand cause and effect regarding behavior and consequences can transfer this to understanding the language of cause and effect in a science experiment using an "if-then" hypothesis structure or a historical narrative seeking to explain the causes and consequences of a war. If a child can compare and contrast dogs and cats, he or she can apply this same mental scheme to comparing and contrasting two systems of government. However, this understanding and the ability to articulate it must be brought to a conscious level. Students might be able to do this in their everyday life but not understand how these structures are transferable to school-based situations. The distinction between conversational language and academic language is more complex than is readily apparent, and these features, too, need to be taught explicitly.

ELLs receiving all-English instruction face a daunting task: learning the regular academic curriculum that all students must learn *while* becoming sufficiently fluent in English so that eventually they can benefit from mainstream English instruction. This is a tall order for students and their teachers. To help address this challenge, educators have devised a number of techniques and strategies designed to make English content area instruction more accessible and meaningful to ELLs to facilitate academic learning and language development. This is a very important—even essential—goal. However, there is little research that has evaluated the impact of these strategies on achievement; we are still a ways from where we can say how—and whether—content area learning *and* academic language development can be accomplished simultaneously so that most English learners are able to keep pace with their English-speaking peers.

Nonetheless, although we lack hard data attesting to their effectiveness, these approaches provide good starting points for educators eager to connect productively with the ELLs in their classes. Practitioners, policy makers, and researchers should then try to determine which of these approaches (and possibly others) actually have the desired effects on ELLs' academic and language learning.

## SCIENCE INSTRUCTION FOR ELLs

A curriculum area that has lately seen considerable activity targeted at ELLs is science. For example, Lee, Deaktor, Hart, Cuevas, and Enders (2005) studied a "science inquiry" approach as part of a research program aimed at teaching science to diverse third and fourth graders, some of whom were

English learners. According to Cuevas, Lee, Hart, and Deaktor (2005), "Science inquiry occurs when students generate questions, plan procedures, design and carry out investigations, analyze data, draw conclusions, and report findings" (p. 342). Researchers helped teachers make the inquiry process explicit for students by developing an inquiry framework, which included pictures illustrating the process. The science lessons also explicitly promoted oral and written English language development. Students wrote expository paragraphs or narrative stories describing scientific processes. Teachers introduced key vocabulary and used multiple modes of communication and representation (e.g., verbal, gestural, graphic, written methods) to assist students' comprehension. Teachers' guides offered additional strategies intended to make the instruction more meaningful and productive: incorporating students' prior linguistic and cultural knowledge into science instruction (for example, science terms in students' L1—Spanish and Haitian Creole); correlations with state science standards and science assessments; transparencies with pictures, tables, graphic organizers, and charts.

After approximately a half year of instruction (2 hours per week), Lee et al. (2005) found that all students—ELL, non-ELL, and students formerly ELL—made significant progress with respect to learning science concepts and improving writing skills. In most cases, test gains for ELLs and non-ELLs were comparable, although the ELLs began and ended the study with significantly lower scores. There was no comparison group, so researchers cannot say to what extent this approach was more effective than a conventional or different approach to science instruction. In a study of a professional development intervention that used the science inquiry model, Lee, Maerten-Rivera, Penfield, LeRoy, and Secada (2008) found similar results: There were achievement gains over the year for both ELLs and non-ELLs, and gains were roughly equivalent or perhaps slightly lower for ELLs. However, although the ELLs made gains similar to that of the non-ELLs, ELL achievement still remained significantly lower.

Students in the intervention schools also had higher achievement than students in comparison schools on a state science test. Unfortunately, there were no pre-intervention achievement data at the two schools, so we do not know how much of the difference can be attributed to the intervention. Moreover, as promising as the science inquiry approach and accompanying professional development seem to be, the program was multifaceted, with numerous elements, and so it is impossible to know what parts of the intervention were responsible for students' science learning over its course.

## RECOMMENDATIONS

- Keep in mind the fundamental challenge ELLs in all-English instruction face: learning academic content while simultaneously becoming increasingly proficient in English. Because of this challenge, we do not know to what extent ELLs can keep pace with English speakers; nonetheless, our goal should be to make academic content as accessible as possible for these students and promote English language development as students learn academic content.

- **Effective teaching for ELLs is similar in many ways to effective teaching for English speakers.** As we saw with literacy instruction, effective teaching in general is probably the foundation of effective teaching for ELLs. As do all learners, ELLs benefit from clear goals and objectives, well-structured tasks, adequate practice, opportunities to interact with others, frequent assessment and reteaching as needed, and other elements of effective instruction identified in the professional and research literature.

- **Sheltered techniques probably help make academic content accessible for English learners while helping promote English language development.** Although effective generic instruction is the foundation for effective teaching of ELLs, it is almost certainly not sufficient. Educators and researchers have devised a number of techniques and strategies that are probably helpful for making academic content accessible to English learners and promoting their English language development (see Box 5.2 and Echevarría et al., 2008). Although our knowledge of which techniques are truly effective is very incomplete, they are the best tools currently available.

- **Implement sheltered strategies in classrooms and evaluate their effectiveness in terms of concrete student outcomes.** Formal research is underway to evaluate the effects of various sheltered strategies. However, educators themselves must help lead the way; there is simply no time to wait until researchers address all of the important issues regarding sheltered instruction.

- **Teach academic language as a key part of content area instruction.** Learning academic language is one of the most pressing challenges ELLs face. Knowledge of academic disciplines—science, social studies, history, and math—is of course what content area instruction is all about. But just as important is the *language* needed to learn about and discuss academic content. Most ELLs eventually acquire adequate conversational language skills, but they often lack the *academic language* skills that are essential for high levels of achievement in the content areas (and for success in school and in any job requiring professional language abilities). Educators must focus on the academic language needed for academic achievement. As with sheltered techniques, we are lacking a solid research base that identifies effective techniques and approaches. There are promising directions, however (e.g., Dutro & Moran, 2001; Lyster, 2007; Schleppegrell, 2001; Zwiers, 2008). Educators are strongly encouraged to learn about them, implement them in their classrooms, and try to determine which best meet the needs of their students.

# REFERENCES

Bailey, A. (Ed.). (2007). *The language demands of school: Putting academic English to the test.* New Haven, CT: Yale University Press.

Baker, C. (2006). *Foundations of bilingual education and bilingualism* (4th ed.). Clevedon, UK: Multilingual Matters.

Berman, P., Minicucci, C., McLaughlin, B., Nelson, B., & Woodworth, K. (1995). *School reform and student diversity: Case studies of exemplary practices for English language learner students.* Santa Cruz, CA: National Center for Research on Cultural Diversity and Second Language Learning, and B.W. Associates.

California Department of Education. (2000). *History-social science content standards for California public schools.* Sacramento: Author. Retrieved from http://www .cde.ca.gov/be/st/ss/index.asp.

Cuevas, P., Lee, O., Hart, J., & Deaktor, R. (2005). Improving science inquiry with elementary students of diverse backgrounds. *Journal of Research in Science Teaching, 42,* 337–357.

Cummins, J. (1979). Cognitive/academic language proficiency, linguistic interdependence, the optimum age question and some other matters. *Working Papers on Bilingualism, 19,* 121–129.

Cummins, J. (1989). *Empowering minority students.* Sacramento, CA: California Association for Bilingual Education.

Droga, L., & Humphrey, S. (2005). *Grammar and meaning: An introduction for primary teachers.* Marrickville, New South Wales, Australia: Target Texts.

Dutro, S., & Moran, C. (2001). Rethinking English language instruction: An architectural approach. In G. García (Ed.), *Reaching the highest level of English literacy* (pp. 227–258). Newark, DE: International Reading Association.

Echevarría, J., Short, D., & Powers, K. (2006). School reform and standards-based education: A model for English-language learners. *The Journal of Educational Research, 99,* 195–210.

Echevarría, J., Vogt, M., & Short, D. (2008). *Making content comprehensible for English learners: The SIOP model* (3rd ed.). Boston: Allyn & Bacon.

Fillmore, L. W., & Snow, C. (2002). What teachers need to know about language. In C. Adger, C. Snow, & D. Christian (Eds.), *What teachers need to know about language* (pp. 7–53). McHenry, IL: Center for Applied Linguistics and Delta Systems.

Genesee, F., Lindholm-Leary, K., Saunders, W., & Christian, D. (2006). *Educating English language learners.* New York: Cambridge University Press.

Hakuta, K., Butler, Y. G., & Witt, D. (2000). *How long does it take English learners to attain proficiency?* Linguistic Minority Research Institute. (ERIC Document Reproduction Service No. FL026180). Available at http://www.lmri .ucsb.edu/publications/00_ /hakuta.pdf.

Halliday, M. (1994). *An introduction to functional grammar* (2nd ed.). London: Edward Arnold.

Krashen, S. D. (2003). *Explorations in language acquisition and use: The Taipei lectures.* Portsmouth, NH: Heinemann.

Lee, O., Deaktor, R., Hart, J., Cuevas, P., & Enders, C. (2005). An instructional intervention's impact on the science and literacy achievement of culturally and linguistically diverse elementary students. *Journal of Research in Science Teaching, 42,* 857–887.

Lee, O., Maerten-Rivera, J., Penfield, R., LeRoy, K., & Secada, W. (2008). Science achievement of English language learners in urban elementary schools: Results of a first-year professional development intervention. *Journal of Research in Science Teaching, 45,* 31–52.

Lyster, R. (2007). *Learning and teaching languages through content: A counterbalanced approach.* Philadelphia: John Benjamins.

Montecel, M. R., & Cortez, J. D. (2002). Successful bilingual education programs: Development and the dissemination of criteria to identify promising and exemplary practices in bilingual education at the national level. *Bilingual Research Journal, 26*, 1–22.

Porter, P. (2007). *Reflections, the United States: Making a nation.* Orlando, FL: Harcourt School Publishers.

Scarcella, R. (2003). *Accelerating academic English: A focus on English language learners.* Oakland: Regents of the University of California.

Schleppegrell, M. J. (2001). Linguistic features of the language of schooling. *Linguistics and Education, 12*, 431–459.

Schleppegrell, M. J., & Achugar, M. (2003). Learning language and learning history: A functional linguistics approach. *TESOL Journal, 12*, 21–27.

University of California, Berkeley History Social Science Project. (2009). *Building academic literacy through history, summer institute.* Berkeley: Regents of University of California.

Zwiers, J. (2008). *Building academic language: Essential practices for content classrooms, grades 5–12.* San Francisco: Jossey-Bass.

# 6

# *School and District Role*

## *Focus and Coherence*

In 1993, Wang, Haertel, and Walberg published a massive synthesis of educational research from around the world and concluded that "distal" factors—state, district, and school policies—did not affect student outcomes as much as "proximal," or classroom-based, factors did. Wang et al. argued that distal factors are steps removed from the daily learning experiences of most students and what affects learning is what students experience most immediately and consistently. They wrote that

- What can schools and districts do to improve ELL achievement?
- How are schoolwide focus and coherence important for improving ELL achievement?
- How can assessment play a role in improving ELL achievement?
- What is the role of school and district leadership in supporting ELL achievement?
- How do we link school and district policies with classroom practice?

> simply instituting new policies whether state, district or school level will not necessarily enhance student learning. . . . Policies do not always reach down to the classroom level. Effective policies require implementation by teachers at the classroom and student level. (p. 276)

Since that time, however, with the emergence of standards-based reform, there have been increased demands to ensure success for all students, leading to high-stakes accountability systems for school, teacher, and pupil performance. As a result, districts are playing an increased role in interpreting and mediating school responses to state and federal policy interventions, and schools are playing a role in mediating teacher responses to district policies. Genesee et al. (2006) argue that classroom practices must be linked to a larger schoolwide or districtwide picture:

> Educators need more than an array of specific methods or activities that they can draw on when planning literacy or academic subjects. They need comprehensive frameworks for selecting, sequencing, and delivering instruction over the course of an entire year and from grade to grade. (p. 231)

Over the past 10 years we have seen increasing attempts at district and school levels to try to provide coherent instruction for English learners through the adoption of consistent programs and approaches (Coleman, 2006). What do we know about the impact of these efforts on the achievement of English learners?

There is a general consensus in the research and professional literature that a sustained and coherent academic focus in schools and districts leads to higher student achievement. Various aspects of school and district functioning, such as leadership, goals, consistent curricula, professional development, ongoing support and supervision, and regular assessments that inform instruction are "levers" school and district administrators can use to help shape the academic experiences of students (see, e.g., Black & Wiliam, 1998; Bliss, Firestone, & Richards, 1991; Edmonds, 1979; Fullan, 2007; Good & Brophy, 1986; Joyce, Showers, & Rolheiser-Bennett, 1987).

But as in many other areas reviewed in this book, when it comes to English learners, we have less research. Specifically, we have less research linking school and district factors to measures of student achievement. Moreover, because of the near absence of experimental research or at least studies that observe changes over time, it is difficult to draw firm conclusions about cause and effect (see Chapter 1). Nonetheless, there is good reason to believe that what gets emphasized in schools and districts will influence— although in no way guarantee—what teachers do and students learn, whether students are English speakers or English learners. As the Center for Research on Education, Diversity and Excellence (CREDE) report concluded:

> Schools with high-quality programs have a cohesive school-site vision, shared goals that define their expectations for achievement, a clear instructional focus on and commitment to achievement, and high expectations. . . . The importance of these characteristics has been found in mainstream schools, low-performing schools, and bilingual programs serving ELLs. (Genesee et al., 2006, p. 186)

In earlier chapters we discussed research on instructional approaches or techniques to improve ELLs' achievement. This chapter discusses the roles of the district and school, as supported by research that links distal (at the school or district levels) to proximal (at the classroom level) influences on student learning. We discuss research on school or district policies such as explicit academic goals for ELLs, ongoing assessment, leadership at the district and school level, and professional development.

## GETTING FROM HERE TO THERE

With a few exceptions, most of the studies that identify school or district factors tell us very little about how to make a school go from less to more effective with its ELL population. They tell us the characteristics of schools considered to be effective with ELLs but not how they got to be that way. In addition, several of the studies report on "exemplary" or "high-quality" programs, but it is unclear what criteria are used to make that determination. Often these schools are nominated by educators who feel the school has a strong or exemplary program, but we do not know whether the achievement of students in the school is any better than the achievement of students in other schools.

Nonetheless, the one thing that seems to surface when we look at the studies as a whole is the importance of a coherent academic program where teachers and administrators focus on doing whatever is necessary to assure the academic achievement of ELLs. In other words, higher achievement levels for ELLs appear to be the result of focused, sustained, and coordinated work among educators committed to the educational success of these students. In her study of eight "exemplary" elementary and middle schools for English language learners, McLeod (1996) makes the following observation:

> In each case the elements fit together like puzzle pieces to form a coherent overall program. Each piece of the puzzle relies on the others for its success. For example, a smooth transition for LEP students from native language or sheltered instruction to all-English instruction depends on collaboration between teachers of LEP students and teachers of English proficient students, which in turn is greatly facilitated by setting aside common planning time during which these teachers regularly confer, which itself relies on a reorganized daily class schedule. (Conclusion section, para. 2)

There are probably numerous ways of accomplishing this sort of coherence, and the studies we review provide some useful clues. Some have examined the effects, over a year or more, of explicit efforts to improve the achievement of ELLs (e.g., Goldenberg, 2004; Livingston & Flaherty, 1997; McDougall, Saunders, & Goldenberg, 2007; Slavin & Madden, 1998).

Others begin by identifying schools and districts that are relatively successful, according to some criteria, then try to figure out what distinguishes them from schools and districts that are less successful (e.g., American Institutes of Research & WestEd, 2006; Lucas, Henze, & Donato, 1990; McLeod, 1996; Reyes, Scribner, & Scribner, 1999; Williams et al., 2007). Taken as a whole, the studies provide some reasonable insights for administrators interested in improving ELLs' achievement in their schools and districts.

## EXPLICIT ACADEMIC GOALS

One way to develop consistency and coherence in schools and districts is to begin with setting explicit academic goals. This was a finding of several of the studies reviewed here. American Institutes of Research and WestEd (2006), for example, found that schools with higher ELL achievement set academic goals by maintaining the following:

- Schoolwide focus on ELD and standards-based instruction
- Shared priorities and expectations in regard to educating English learners
- Curriculum and instruction targeted to English learners' progress

Similarly, Williams et al. (2007) found that schools with higher ELL achievement levels had "a coherent, standards-based curriculum." Teachers at these schools reported that their school had identified essential standards that guided classroom instruction. Their schools also used pacing guides that help teachers stay "on track" and cover course content in a timely fashion. Principals at schools where ELLs had the highest achievement reported that the district had "a coherent grade-by-grade curriculum [and] expected its principals to ensure that curriculum was implemented" (American Institutes of Research and WestEd, 2006, p. 9).

Studies reported by Goldenberg (2004), McDougall et al. (2007), and Saunders, Goldenberg, and Gallimore (2009) are informative on this point because they are the only ones where faculties and administrators worked to set explicit schoolwide academic goals for students. Student learning goals need not be made up from thin air. In the project reported in McDougall et al. and Saunders et al., published state standards were the starting point for the explicit student learning goals around which faculties and administrators focused their efforts. Over a period of several years, school achievement improved in absolute terms and in comparison to the rest of the district.

Schools that use Success for All (Slavin & Madden, 1998) do not engage in a goal-setting process as do the schools that use the Getting Results model reported by Goldenberg (2004), McDougall et al. (2007), and Saunders et al. (2009). But Success for All comes with its own curriculum, curriculum materials, and curriculum-embedded assessments, so academic goals are implicit in this whole-school intervention. Success for All (see Chapter 3) is perhaps the most successful of the whole-school reform models of the 1990s and has shown positive achievement effects with ELLs (Dianda & Flaherty, 1995; Livingston & Flaherty, 1997; Slavin & Madden, 1998).

# ONGOING STUDENT ASSESSMENT

Explicit and agreed-upon goals are probably important for achieving substantive improvements because they are vital for maintaining a coherent and stable student-centered vision. Assessments that then measure ongoing progress toward agreed-upon goals—often referred to as "formative assessments"—reinforce the importance of the goals and help teachers and administrators gauge their goal-directed efforts. This finding has been one of the most common in the literature on school effectiveness, and it has been reported in the research we review here on ELLs: Consistent use of achievement indicators to track student progress is related to improvements in student outcomes (Black & Wiliam, 1998). For example, Success for All (Dianda & Flaherty, 1995; Livingston & Flaherty, 1997; Slavin & Madden, 1998) uses systematic and regular student assessment. Regular and systematic student assessment—explicitly linked to schoolwide goals—is also a key aspect of Getting Results (Goldenberg, 2004; McDougall et al., 2007; Saunders et al., 2009), which had a positive impact on student achievement.

Correlational research by American Institutes of Research and WestEd (2006) and Williams et al. (2007) found that ELLs who attend schools that regularly assess academic progress have higher achievement than ELLs who do not attend schools that assess regularly. Williams et al. found that "prioritizing student achievement by using measurable and monitored objectives" (p. 10) was the single most important factor that distinguished schools with relatively higher-achieving ELLs from schools with lower-achieving ELLs. Similarly, American Institutes of Research and WestEd report that "ongoing assessment coupled with data-driven decision making" (p. 9) was one of the distinguishing characteristics of higher-achieving schools. High-achieving districts, for their part, provided "assistance to schools in analyzing data" (p. 9).

Educators need comprehensive frameworks to provide continuous, coherent, and developmentally appropriate educational interventions. This is absolutely critical if ELLs are to be successful. One of the ways to assure that students receive such a program and, most important, benefit from it, is to monitor progress on a regular basis. We are not referring to standardized and high-stakes assessments but rather to instructionally illuminating assessments that provide teachers with timely feedback about the effects of instruction on student growth and learning. Information from these assessments then informs instructional decisions for students.

Box 6.1 shows how one school used assessment to inform instruction.

**Box 6.1**

### Using Assessment to Inform Instruction Scenario

The principal, the ELL coach, and the teachers at Riverside School identify student learning needs by looking at formative assessments (which all teachers give four times a year) and, to some extent, state assessment scores. Assessments also help them to identify professional development needs. The fall formative assessments revealed that early advanced and even advanced ELLs in the upper grades were weak in general academic vocabulary (e.g., *analyze, abandon, suspicious*) and content-specific vocabulary (e.g., *society, climate, evolution*). Among beginning and early intermediate students in the early grades, verb tenses needed work.

The teachers have weekly one-hour grade-level meetings focused on one topic, based on the formative assessments, such as strategies to teach students to speak in the future tense or lessons to develop vocabulary to teach important academic words that will come up in the next social studies unit. Teachers do some of their planning together and arrange for small-group instruction based on students' proficiency levels as determined by the formative assessment results.

They will then teach the lessons and bring back student work to discuss and analyze results with colleagues at the next meeting. They do this routinely, working systematically over time to improve student learning in identified areas. The formative assessments help them track their progress.

## LEADERSHIP

Leadership is another school attribute and, to a lesser degree, district attribute that has been associated with higher student achievement. A school or district can increase the chances of program success if it puts the full force of its resources behind that program. Districts communicate what they most value by what they give attention to and require. Assembling and deploying resources and effectively communicating values and priorities requires effective leadership. When it is present, it is more likely that what is valued will be reflected in what is taught in the classroom (Coleman, 2006).

McDougall et al. (2007) found that implementation of the Getting Results school change model was dependent upon the organizational and educational leadership provided by the school principal. Active principal engagement and a clear indication that change efforts were a priority were essential to success. McDougall et al. found that

> principals at most GR [Getting Results] schools demonstrated greater awareness, focus, and participation in the day-to-day

academic plans and actions of teachers at each grade level. The tighter academic linkages between teachers and administrators at GR schools facilitated more effective execution of goal-directed plans than at comparison schools, where the evaluator observed more frequent "slippage" between intended actions and actual implementation of academic initiatives. (p. 70)

The importance of leadership became clear in Goldenberg's (2004) case study of successful change at one school. When leadership support for the school improvement efforts disappeared, student achievement fell below levels of the year in which reform was initiated. As funding ended and key participants left, new district priorities took over, and school staff went on to other projects.

District leaders and school principals who have a sincere desire to help English learners succeed, and have done everything they know how to do, are frequently frustrated when they don't see the fruits of their labors. With the added incentive of raising English learners' subgroup test scores under No Child Left Behind, districts are taking unprecedented measures to address ELL needs. This has resulted in districtwide efforts to implement approaches and programs with a coherent focus (Coleman, 2006). American Institutes of Research and WestEd (2006) found that when districts and schools have focused leadership that communicates and makes sure all staff members understand the focus and priorities for ELLs, schools and districts have higher achievement among the ELL students. Williams et al. (2007) echoed this theme; they, too, found that ELL achievement was higher when school and district administrators provided focused and sustained leadership around ELL instructional issues:

> Principal leadership is being redefined to focus on effective management of the school improvement process. . . . District leadership, accountability, and support appear to influence ELL student achievement as well. (p. 12)

But leadership is not solely the domain of administrators; leadership from teachers—including instructional specialists (cf. August & Shanahan, 2006)—is also essential. The success of the Getting Results model (Goldenberg, 2004; McDougall et al., 2007; Saunders et al., 2009) required teachers to take leadership roles in grade-level and planning meetings and informally in other settings. Teacher leadership was essential for helping colleagues and holding them accountable for working toward agreed-upon student learning goals. Teacher expertise was also essential, and leadership created the opportunities for expertise to find its way into schools (Goldenberg, 2004). We revisit this topic next, in "Professional Development."

## PROFESSIONAL DEVELOPMENT

Professional development is a fourth school and district factor associated with higher achievement for ELLs. Both the National Literacy Panel (NLP) and the CREDE reports take strong positions on this point. For schools to be effective with ELLs, there must be sustained and focused professional development:

> Attention needs to be paid to teachers, including their levels and kinds of professional development, their understanding of different instructional and assessment approaches, their knowledge and application of second-language acquisition theory, and the processes that are required to ensure that new teachers acquire competence in using new approaches. (Genesee et al., 2006, p. 232)

The NLP cites research suggesting that professional development can be thought of as producing three different kinds of changes: changes in teachers' classroom practices, in their beliefs and attitudes, and in students' learning outcomes. This research suggests that changes are not "unidirectional"; in other words, we do not necessarily know whether changes in beliefs and attitudes lead to changes in practices or the other way around. Practice and belief is a case of the chicken and the egg. Although some researchers suggest that changing teachers' beliefs is the first step in the process of changing practice (Richardson, 1991), Calderón and Marsh (1988) found that changing teacher practices and producing what they perceived to be positive student outcomes changed teachers' beliefs. In other words, teachers may be asked to implement practices they don't believe in and therefore would not have tried. Being required and supported to do so, they might find those practices are in fact effective and change their beliefs and expectations for students as a result.

Goldenberg and Gallimore (1991), Goldenberg (2004), McDougall et al. (2007), and Saunders et al. (2009) found this in their studies of schools improving over time. Teachers' beliefs and expectations about student learning changed as teachers' practices changed; teachers began observing results they had previously not seen, which then had the effect of raising their expectations for what students could actually accomplish. Many teachers were initially skeptical of curricular and instructional changes intended to present students with more challenging material that would bring them up to grade level. They changed their expectations, however, as practices and achievement changed. McDougall et al. report that the schoolwide effort to improve teaching and learning

> fostered a group ethos among [teachers]—a collective willingness and commitment to formulate, adapt, implement, and evaluate instructional processes that targeted student achievement. (p. 74)

Through collaborative goal setting, analysis of indicators, and reflection on teacher-controlled instructional variables, [it] impacted teachers' expectations for student achievement. (p. 77)

The following scenario describes how one school principal provided ongoing professional development and coaching to the teachers.

---

**Box 6.2**

### Ongoing Professional Development Scenario

Mr. G. teaches first grade at Buena Vista Elementary School, which is collaborating with two faculty members at a state university on a grant focused on promoting early literacy development among English learners. The purpose of the project, initiated by the principal in collaboration with several interested teachers, is to develop a coaching model that will help consultants and teachers work together to improve early literacy attainment for ELLs.

The teachers first attended a half-day session where the university faculty explained the goals of the project and solicited the participation of the K–2 teachers. Following the half-day kickoff, teachers began to attend monthly training sessions conducted by the university faculty; they were also observed once a month by the researcher or consultant. There are precoaching and postcoaching conferences before and after the observations. In between trainings, teachers meet in grade-level teams to work on agreed-upon goals for student learning. The principal makes sure these meetings are regular weekly events by hiring two experienced aides to take each grade level for PE so that teachers are free to meet during this time.

The principal makes clear his expectation that teachers are to focus on specific instructional issues at these meetings. Teachers and researchers together identified specific learning goals for students. They track student progress using formative assessments, systematic teacher observations, and collection of student work.

---

Calderón and Marsh (1988) highlight the importance of ongoing staff development that builds on theory, effective teacher craft, and close collaboration between researchers and teachers. They studied the impact of "trainer of trainer institutes" throughout California on bilingual teachers and other school personnel from 1980 to 1986. Three different cohorts each attended 12–15 days a year for three years. Administrators supported the bilingual program and funded 95 percent of the cost.

To make sure new strategies were used in the classroom, the institute (a) integrated theory and research on oral language reading and writing with demonstrations of specific teaching models in different contexts,

(b) introduced participants to principles of effective professional development, (c) provided time for practice of the instructional models at the training sessions (with feedback and extensive support), and (d) encouraged the use of new models in the classroom through coaching checklists and collection of information about implementation. Observation and coaching protocols were used to help teachers identify areas needing assistance. Teachers acquired leadership skills and the skills to coach other teachers. Presenting theory, modeling the strategies, and giving teachers the opportunity to practice with feedback provided an effective professional development model. Importantly, however, the shortcomings that were ranked most troublesome by the participants were lack of administrative support for peer coaching and inadequate administrative knowledge of bilingual instruction and supervisory skills (August & Shanahan, 2006, pp. 558–559).

Calderón and Marsh (1988) did not demonstrate a direct link between professional development and improved student achievement (indeed, none of the professional development studies reviewed by the NLP reported effects on student outcomes), but American Institutes of Research and WestEd (2006) and Williams et al. (2007) both report that a focus on professional development at the school and district levels was associated with higher ELL achievement. Neither study went into depth at individual schools nor about any particular professional development models, but their findings indicated that principals in schools with higher-achieving ELLs made sure their staffs had "instructional expertise and skills to address ELL needs," and high-achieving districts made sure there was adequate "professional development and technical assistance related to ELL education" (American Institutes of Research & WestEd, 2006, p. 9). Williams et al. (2007) also found that schools and districts that "encourage teacher collaboration and build educator capacity" (p. 10) had somewhat higher ELL achievement than schools where "building teacher capacity" was not a priority.

The study by Echevarría, Short, and Powers (2006) that was discussed in Chapter 5 found a modest link between professional development and student achievement. The researchers trained 19 teachers (in six different schools) in the SIOP instructional model and found a small improvement in the quality of expository writing produced by their middle-school ELLs, compared with students of similar backgrounds whose teachers had not received the training (four teachers in two different schools). Impact on student achievement was small but statistically significant.

Saunders et al. (2009) report a much more substantial impact of a whole-school improvement effort that included school-based professional development where teachers worked collaboratively over time and learned to address specific instructional challenges they faced. In a separate publication, Gallimore, Ermeling, Saunders, and Goldenberg (2009) refer to this approach as "moving the learning of teaching closer to practice." The approach produced quite large improvements in achievement at the majority-ELL schools, compared to comparison schools and the district overall. The professional development was highly contextualized within a comprehensive effort to improve achievement, which included setting clear goals for students' learning, regular assessments to gauge progress, effective school and grade-level leadership, assistance from outside consultants, and stable, consistent settings where teachers could come together to work on improving their instruction and students' learning. It is probably impossible to determine the impact of any one component, but qualitative data suggest teachers highly valued (and benefited from) the professional development aspects. Readers can see videos of teacher meetings, classroom instruction, and teacher reflections on the process at http://www.stanford.edu/~claudeg/CD1/getting_results/index.html.

Findings from Williams et al. (2007) about the relationship between teacher certification and ELL achievement strike a more cautious note, however. California (the site of the study) requires all teachers who become credentialed to receive at least some training in English language development (see Chapter 4), sheltered instruction (see Chapter 5), and other topics thought to be important for the education of ELLs. Sixty-nine percent of the teachers in the 237 elementary schools in the study had this credential. (This is a relatively new requirement, so not all teachers had this special authorization when study data were collected by Williams et al.) Williams et al. found that whether a school had a high or low percentage of teachers with this ELL credential made no difference in the achievement of ELLs at the school. There are many possible explanations for this, but one possibility is that we simply do not yet have a good handle on what generalized teacher training—as opposed to very contextualized training specific to the instructional issues teachers face daily—is most helpful for the education of ELLs.

## OTHER SCHOOL AND DISTRICT FACTORS

Numerous other school and district factors have been cited by different studies as important for promoting ELLs' achievement:

- American Institutes of Research and WestEd (2006) and Williams et al. (2007) found that *adequate resources* to support the academic program distinguished more and less effective schools for ELLs; in the Williams et al. study, teacher and principal reports about "availability of resources" were the second-most important factor (after use of assessment data) distinguishing more and less effective schools.
- American Institutes of Research and WestEd (2006) and Williams et al. (2007) also found that *parent and community outreach and involvement* differentiated between more and less effective schools;

in the Williams et al. study, this factor was the least important of seven factors that distinguished more and less effective schools for ELLs.

- Genesee et al. (2006) report a diverse group of studies whose conclusions support the importance of *a culture of high expectations*. Such a culture has many dimensions, including belief by staff that all children can learn; a positive, orderly, safe, caring school environment that facilitates learning; a meaningful, challenging, and enriched (not remedial) curriculum; curriculum grounded in sound theory and best practices; consistent and sustained programs; and programs where ELLs and non-ELLs are integrated.

## LINKING SCHOOL AND DISTRICT POLICIES WITH CLASSROOM PRACTICE

The emergence of whole-school change models has changed the way we look at the connection between policy and classroom practices. Creating a change in classroom practice is a time-consuming process that requires considerable investment on the part of the change agents. Efforts can take one to three years and involve trainings and workshops, meetings, intensive summer programs, and classroom follow-ups. Studies reviewed here suggest that intensive professional development is necessary, but it cannot be of the one-shot workshop variety. Instead, it must be embedded in the work lives of teachers and the routines of teaching. Professional development needs to be ongoing and consist of (1) presentations and meetings with teachers and those providing the professional development, (2) classroom practice coupled with coaching and feedback, and (3) teacher learning communities where teachers can work with and discuss ongoing challenges, issues, and successes with colleagues. Some of the studies reviewed here also involved close outside collaborations with university researchers (August & Shanahan, 2006).

Goldenberg and Gallimore (1991), for example, examined changes that occurred in Benson Elementary School, with a 90 percent Hispanic student enrollment. The staff at Benson worked together over a three-year period to improve early Spanish reading achievement. According to the authors, the changes were not the result of implementing a particular model or program; rather they can be characterized as a "shift in the school's early literacy culture that transformed norms and expectations" (p. 4). The shift came about as a result of early primary teachers working together to improve beginning Spanish reading at the school. In follow-up studies at other schools, Goldenberg (2004) and McDougall et al. (2007) document changes at similar elementary schools where teachers worked with university collaborators to improve teaching and learning. The end results were substantial improvement in students' literacy attainment (Saunders et al., 2009).

A very different model is provided by Success for All (Livingston & Flaherty, 1997; Slavin & Madden, 1998). As discussed earlier, Success for All comprises a number of components, such as a well-structured and well-designed curriculum, explicit instructional models, and effective school and classroom organization strategies. Success for All also uses an effective and fairly well-established (see Joyce, Showers, & Rolheiser-Bennett, 1987) professional development model whereby trainers provide three days of training on curriculum and instruction prior to the start of school, followed by classroom visits to provide teachers and administrators with feedback and coaching as needed. As new program components are introduced, trainers provide additional trainings and follow-up observations.

These studies demonstrate the progress schools can achieve when staffs work together to address specific issues, although in all cases assistance from an external support person (consultant or advisor) was essential for the process. The studies highlight the importance of mobilizing school staffs to focus on the needs of language-minority students and provide evidence that a concerted school effort involving outside agents (researchers or consultants) and school personnel (principals, specialists, and classroom teachers) can make a difference. They also point to the importance of sustained and comprehensive efforts. Language-minority students, especially those who live in difficult economic circumstances, face many challenges. Improving school- and districtwide achievement will undoubtedly require comprehensive and multifaceted solutions.

## RECOMMENDATIONS

Consistent and coherent district- and schoolwide policies will help build an effective program for ELLs. These policies and practices include the following:

- School and district administrators (and all personnel dedicated to ELLs) with ELL expertise and who are current on the research on improving ELLs' achievement; these administrators are best able to make informed choices about programs, policies, and practices that are likely to influence students' school success
- Clear and challenging academic goals for students, explicitly articulated and understood by all teachers and embedded in well-structured curriculum
- Support for coherence from school to school, grade to grade, and class to class regarding the selection, sequencing, and delivery of instruction; accountability measures, such as implementation checklists, will be more useful if there is general buy-in among administrators and staff
- Ongoing, systematic assessment that provides teachers with timely information about how students are progressing with respect to these academic goals; uniform accountability systems measuring student outcomes in academic subjects and English language development

- Effective, visible, engaged leadership that articulates at every opportunity the importance of providing challenging and meaningful learning opportunities for students
- Ongoing professional development (provided from within school staffs or by outside trainers) focused on helping teachers achieve the learning goals for students
- Professional development supported by routine and systematic collaboration among teachers focused on achieving specific academic goals with students
- Adequate resources to support the academic program
- Parent involvement and community outreach to support the academic program
- A culture of high expectations and accountability at all levels supported by tangible steps to help teachers accomplish instructional goals for students

# REFERENCES

American Institutes for Research & WestEd (2006). *Effects of the implementation of Proposition 227 on the education of English learners, K–12: Findings from a five-year evaluation.* Washington, DC: American Institutes for Research.

August, D., & Shanahan, T. (Eds.). (2006). *Developing literacy in second-language learners: Report of the National Literacy Panel on language-minority children and youth.* Mahwah, NJ: Lawrence Erlbaum.

Black, P., & Wiliam, D. (1998). Assessment and classroom learning. *Assessment in Education: Principles, Policy and Practice, 5,* 7–74.

Bliss, J., Firestone, W., & Richards, C. (Eds.). (1991). *Rethinking effective schools: Research and practice.* Englewood Cliffs, NJ: Prentice Hall.

Calderón, M., & Marsh, D. (1988). Applying research on effective bilingual instruction in a multi-district inservice teacher training program. *NABE Journal, 12,* 133–152.

Coleman, R. (2006). *The role of school districts in the selection and support of English language development programs and approaches.* Unpublished doctoral dissertation, University of Southern California, Los Angeles.

Dianda, M. R., & Flaherty, J. F. (1995). *Report on workstation uses: Effects of Success for All on the reading achievement of first graders in California bilingual programs* (No. 91002006). Los Alamitos, CA: Southwest Regional Laboratory. (ERIC Document Reproduction Service No. ED394327)

Echevarría, J., Short, D., & Powers, K. (2006). School reform and standards-based education: A model for English-language learners. *The Journal of Educational Research, 99,* 195–210.

Edmonds, R. (1979). Effective schools for the urban poor. *Educational Leadership, 37,* 15–27.

Fullan, M. (2007). *The new meaning of educational change* (4th ed.). New York: Teachers College Press.

Gallimore, R., Ermeling, B., Saunders, W., & Goldenberg, C. (2009). Moving the learning of teaching closer to practice: Teacher education implications of school-based inquiry teams. *The Elementary School Journal, 109,* 537–553.

Genesee, F., Lindholm-Leary, K., Saunders, W., & Christian, D. (2006). *Educating English language learners.* New York: Cambridge University Press.

Goldenberg, C. (2004). *Successful school change: Creating settings to improve teaching and learning.* New York: Teachers College Press.

Goldenberg, C., & Gallimore, R. (1991). Local knowledge, research knowledge, and educational change: A case study of first-grade Spanish reading improvement. *Educational Researcher, 20*(8), 2–14.

Good, T., & Brophy, J. (1986). School effects. In M. Wittrock (Ed.), *Handbook of research on teaching* (3rd ed., pp. 570–602). New York: Macmillan.

Joyce, B., Showers, B., & Rolheiser-Bennett, C. (1987). Staff development and student learning: A synthesis of research on models of teaching. *Educational Leadership, 45,* 11–23.

Livingston, M., & Flaherty, J. (1997). *Effects of Success for All on reading achievement in California schools.* Los Alamitos, CA: WestEd.

Lucas, T., Henze, R., & Donato, R. (1990). Promoting the success of Latino language-minority students: An exploratory study of six high schools. *Harvard Educational Review, 60,* 315–340.

McDougall, D., Saunders, W. M., & Goldenberg, C. (2007). Inside the black box of school reform: Explaining the how and why of change at Getting Results schools. *International Journal of Disability, Development and Education, 54,* 51–89.

McLeod, B. (1996). *School reform and student diversity: Exemplary schooling for language minority students.* NCBE Resource Colection Series, No. 4. Retrieved December 26, 2008, at http://www.ncela.gwu.edu.

Reyes, P., Scribner, J., & Scribner, A. (Eds.). (1999). *Lessons from high-performing Hispanic schools.* New York: Teachers College Press.

Richardson, V. (1991). Significant and worthwhile change in teaching practice. *Educational Researcher, 19*(7), 10–18.

Saunders, W., Goldenberg, C., & Gallimore, R. (2009). Increasing achievement by focusing grade level teams on improving classroom learning: A prospective, quasi-experimental study of Title I schools. *American Educational Research Journal, 46,* 1006–1033.

Slavin, R. E., & Madden, N. A. (1998). *Success for all/Éxito para todos: Effects on the reading achievement of students acquiring English* (Report No. 19). Baltimore: The Johns Hopkins University, Center for Research on the Education of Students Placed at Risk.

Wang, M., Haertel, G., & Walberg, H. (1993). Toward a knowledge base for school learning. *Review of Educational Research, 63,* 249–294.

Williams, T., Hakuta, K., Haertel, E., et al. (2007). *Similar English learner students, different results: Why do some schools do better? A follow-up analysis, based on a large-scale survey of California elementary schools serving low-income and EL students.* Mountain View, CA: EdSource.

# 7

# Social, Cultural, and Family Influences

Thus far we have discussed what we know from research on language of instruction and effective instructional practices to promote language, literacy, and academic development of ELLs. We turn now to a somewhat different set of factors: social, cultural, and family influences on ELLs' learning.

English language learners and their families, of course, speak a

- What factors determine or influence a person's sociocultural background?
- Why is it so complex to determine the impact of sociocultural factors on school achievement?
- What is the evidence for the impact of "culturally compatible" instruction on ELL achievement?
- In what two areas is the evidence strongest for the impact of sociocultural factors on ELL achievement?
- For these two areas, what are the most important findings from the research?

language other than English at home. But that is not all that distinguishes them from English speakers. ELLs also come from different social and cultural (or sociocultural) backgrounds. What does this mean? It's a difficult question to answer succinctly, but generally this refers to the social contexts in which children and youth live and go to school. These contexts are defined, or influenced, by such things as a group's beliefs, attitudes, behaviors, and practices, which are often related to their social and political circumstances, their material (or economic) resources, or their ethnic, cultural, or national origin and identity. Any of these factors, and in virtually any combination, can constitute sociocultural influences and define a particular sociocultural group. Most of these factors are not static. With the exception, for example, of national origin (where you were born will always remain where you were born, unless political boundaries shift), these sociocultural characteristics can be at least somewhat dynamic (Goldenberg & Gallimore, 1995). Attitudes, beliefs, practices, economic circumstances, even with whom you identify can shift over a person's life and across generations, thereby shifting—sometimes subtly, sometimes not—a person's or family's sociocultural group membership. Together, this complex array of factors (or influences) creates various and complex sociocultural contexts. These contexts then can influence how students learn or their motivation or their attitudes, which can then in turn influence school achievement. Researching the effects of sociocultural factors on student achievement has posed a large number of challenges, not the least of which has been defining what we mean by sociocultural factors and disentangling their effects on one another and on important outcomes such as school achievement. (Readers who wish to pursue this topic in greater detail are encouraged to consult Cole, 1995; Durán, 1983; Forman, Minick, & Stone, 1993; Jacob & Jordan, 1987; Tharp, 1989.)

## CULTURE AND ACHIEVEMENT AMONG ELLs

We know that different sociocultural groups tend to behave differently, share different beliefs and customs, and have different sorts of experiences they bring with them to school (see Rueda, August, & Goldenberg, 2006). We also know there are differences in achievement among different groups of students: Students from low socioeconomic families tend to do more poorly academically than students from higher socioeconomic families (Sirin, 2005). Students from language-minority backgrounds tend to achieve at lower levels than students from language-majority backgrounds (see Chapter 1). There are also achievement differences among various language-minority groups. Students from homes where Spanish is spoken tend to have lower achievement than students from homes where an Asian language is spoken (National Center for Education Statistics, 1992). Even among Asian students, there are also differences in achievement for students from different national-origin groups—Chinese-, Korean-, and Japanese-descent students have higher achievement than students of Cambodian, Vietnamese, and Laotian descent (Ima & Rumbaut, 1989).

A great many exceptions exist to these generalizations, and no one should ever presume to know anything definitive about someone based on the individual's sociocultural group membership—however we define it. But as generalizations go, different groups do have different customs, beliefs, and behaviors on the one hand and different overall achievement levels on the other. Are the two related, that is, do group characteristics (customs, beliefs, behavior) lead to differences in achievement? Or, more generally, are certain sociocultural characteristics related to differences in school achievement? It is certainly plausible. Consider the following scenarios:

- Students from a particular sociocultural group are more reticent and therefore behave in such a way that teachers do not realize what these students know; teachers then develop lower expectations or teach them less challenging material, which then can depress their achievement.
- Students from another sociocultural group are not used to being in discussions where adults control who gets to talk and for how long; these students might be less likely to participate or may even actively resist participating in a situation in which they feel they have no right to determine when to speak and when to just listen.
- In general, students respond more positively when reading about or presented with materials that are culturally familiar to them; this is typically not an issue with majority-culture students, since by default school instructional materials draw heavily from the majority culture. But for minority-group children, never seeing themselves or their cultures reflected in school could be alienating and depress their achievement.

Readers might be surprised to learn, however, that the evidence to support the proposition that culturally compatible instruction enhances the achievement of English learners is limited. It is certainly plausible and makes a great deal of intuitive sense. But the research is surprisingly thin. Still, the idea that classroom instruction and student sociocultural characteristics should be brought into close alignment has been a prominent theme in professional writing that addresses the education of linguistically, culturally, and ethnically diverse populations. Consider the following excerpts:

Only when teachers understand the cultural backgrounds of their students can they avoid . . . culture clash. In the meantime, the ways in which teachers comprehend and react to students' culture, language, and behaviors may create problems. (ASCD Advisory Panel on Improving Student Achievement, 1995, p. 10)

The challenge for educators is to identify critical differences between and within ethnic minority groups and to incorporate this information into classroom practice. (Sue & Padilla, 1986, p. 62)

Research has shown that students learn more when their classrooms are compatible with their own cultural and linguistic

experience. . . . [Students' learning] is disrupted when the norms
of interaction and communication in a classroom are very different from those to which the student has been accustomed.
(Saravia-Shore & García, 1995, p. 57)

Children whose language and culture do not match those of the
schools are usually forced to adjust their schema. . . . Such negation
of a child's language and culture also negates the child's cognitive
tools and can seriously hinder cognitive development. . . . Effective
instruction of language-minority students includes . . . teaching
practices that take advantage of students' cultural backgrounds.
(E. García, 1994, p. 175)

Their plausibility and intuitive appeal aside, what is the evidence for
these statements?

## EVIDENCE ON CULTURALLY COMPATIBLE
## INSTRUCTION FOR ELLs IS MIXED

*Culture* is a very familiar term that is commonly used, but its meaning is
elusive. A dictionary definition of *culture* is "the sum total of ways of living built up by a group of human beings, which is transmitted from one
generation to another" (*American College Dictionary*, 1968), so the term is
very broad.

The concept of "culture" is very broad, but in many educational writings
and in common everyday use, culture often means a student's "natal"
culture—that is, the ethnic or national-origin culture into which a person is
born. We think of students from the Mexican or Filipino or Khmer culture.
The natal culture is of course an important influence on students' behaviors,
values, motivations, and perhaps even their ways of thinking. The influence
of culture on the educational process is then presumed to be so great that
educators are told, as the quotes above illustrate, that they must take into
account students' culture as they design curriculum and plan instruction;
otherwise they "can seriously hinder cognitive development" (E. García,
1994, p. 175). But the evidence is weak in many respects for ELLs.

In fact, a study reviewed by the National Literacy Panel (NLP) found that
a mastery learning/direct instruction approach (consistent with many of the
instructional principles discussed in Chapters 3–5) produced better effects on
Mexican American students' reading comprehension than did an approach
tailored to students' sociocultural characteristics and learning styles. Another
study,[1] an evaluation of an ambitious federally funded project in the early
1970s (The Edgewood School Plan), found no effects of a comprehensive

---

[1]This study was not reviewed by the NLP since it did not fit its search parameters. The
account reported here is based on Carter and Segura (1979).

program designed to eliminate "cultural incompatibilities" between Mexican-origin students and the schools they attended. Evaluators concluded that the Latino students were "similar to other students in psychosocial aspects" and that "measured academic achievement was not improved by four years of treatment" (Carter & Segura, 1979, p. 320).

Some studies reviewed by the NLP, most of which are methodologically weak, have concluded that culturally accommodated instruction can promote *engagement* and *higher-level participation during lessons*. By far the strongest and most influential of these studies was conducted by Au and Mason (1981). Au and Mason found that when Hawaiian children (whose native language is Hawaiian Creole) were able to speak freely and spontaneously without waiting for teacher permission—an interaction pattern similar to what they were used to at home—their engagement during a reading lesson increased, as did their on-topic and correct responses, the number of ideas they expressed, and the logical inferences they made during the lesson.

This is a meaningful finding, to be sure. Active engagement and the other academically oriented behaviors during the lesson can be important contributors to academic achievement. In addition, these behaviors might indicate increased motivation or an increased sense of connectedness between students and the classroom, both of which are obviously important.

But they are not the same as achievement. Au and Mason (1981) did not provide any gauge of actual learning. Students were engaged in more substantive ways during the lesson itself, but then what was the impact on their comprehension of the story or on the development of reading skills? The fact is, we don't know. The connection Au and Mason demonstrated between culturally accommodated instruction and engagement and participation during a reading lesson is not the same thing as establishing a connection between culturally accommodated instruction and student *learning*. We literally have no idea what students walked away with from the lesson: Did they understand the story better? Did their reading improve? Did their motivation or interest in reading improve? Did they develop more advanced reading strategies? We just can't say. The distinction between engagement and learning is not trivial. At a minimum, educators should understand clearly what this study found and what it did not.

This was a common problem the NLP found: Many of the studies the panel reviewed on the topic of sociocultural influences on achievement—particularly those attempting to make the case for culturally accommodated instruction—failed to gauge student outcomes in *any* way. Critics of the NLP have complained that only experimental studies were considered for the analysis of sociocultural influences. This is untrue; in fact, qualitative studies included in the NLP analysis are discussed below. The problem with many studies in this area is not that they are not experiments; it's that (a) they fail to collect outcome data of any sort and then (b) don't attempt to make explicit (qualitative or quantitative) data-based connections between sociocultural factors and some sort of student outcome.

The key distinction the NLP made in drawing its conclusions about sociocultural influences was not between experimental and nonexperimental studies; it was between studies that gauged student literacy outcomes and studies that did not. Outcomes were defined in the broadest possible way—any gauge, quantitative or qualitative, of achievement or motivation or any other meaningful educational outcome. "Outcomes" could include behavioral observations, student writing, and motivational measures. It was not limited to cognitive or academic measures such as standardized or other types of tests.

Studies in this area often describe different learning contexts for ELLs, either at home or school, and make judgments about whether differences between them might harm student learning. Alternatively, some describe situations where educators bring home and school cultures into alignment, thereby (such is the claim) creating more positive learning environments for students. An example of such a study is one by McCarty, Wallace, Lynch, and Benally (1991), who report on the implementation of an inquiry curriculum for ELL Navajo students that the authors argue is more compatible than the typical school curriculum, with the inductive-inquiry learning pattern children experience in their natal settings. The curriculum was developed around the concept of "k'é, meaning kinship, clanship, and 'right and respectful relations with others and with nature'" (p. 46). The curriculum sequence was

> organized around concepts relevant to k'é, which expand in spiraling fashion to higher levels of abstraction, generality, and complexity. . . . At higher levels, students have opportunities to develop an increasingly sophisticated and critical understanding of the concept in light of interactions of groups of people, nations, and governments. (p. 46)

This study is similar to that of Au and Mason (1981) in that the authors hypothesize that when teachers use culturally familiar interaction styles with students, students are engaged more productively in lessons. But unlike Au and Mason, McCarty et al. (1991) only present a general description of an instructional approach, which they claim is more compatible with the students' home culture, then state that the Native American students in the study responded eagerly and verbally to questioning during the highly interactive lessons in their second language (English). Unlike Au and Mason, McCarty et al. report virtually no data; they simply make assertions.

The claims made by this and other studies reviewed by the NLP about sociocultural influences on the learning and achievement process are certainly plausible. But without actually collecting student outcome data (learning, motivation, or any outcome indicator) that can then be linked to sociocultural influences, there is not even a chance to address the question of whether learning contexts that are accommodated to students' culture will improve student achievement. In contrast, as we discussed earlier, two studies that explicitly put this question to the test suggest the answer is that they will not. At a minimum we can say the issue is far from settled.

We wish to be clear that we are not endorsing teachers' being uninformed about their students' cultures or backgrounds. To the contrary, we encourage educators to read widely, get to know families and community members, and inform themselves of the varieties of human experiences, including (or maybe especially) those of their students. A broad perspective and understanding of different cultures, ways of life, and histories of different peoples should simply be part of what it means to be educated. But educators should not assume that students' sociocultural group membership provides ready guidelines, much less prescriptions, for educational practice.

## USING MATERIAL WITH FAMILIAR CONTENT

There were two areas where the NLP found evidence that bridging home-school cultures—or stated differently, taking into account student sociocultural characteristics—could affect ELL students' achievement. One area has to do with using literacy materials containing familiar content. The other is the influence of parents and families, which we discuss in the next section.

The NLP reviewed a group of studies that make the case that language-minority students' literacy achievement is enhanced when they read or use materials that, although in the second language, have familiar content. Conversely, unfamiliar content can undermine reading comprehension or literacy achievement more generally. These conclusions come from different kinds of studies with second-language learners in different countries.

One study with Arab-speaking students learning Hebrew as a second language found that culturally familiar (Arabic content) reading material in Hebrew led to better reading comprehension among 15- to 16-year-old Druze (Arab) students than did reading material with Jewish content. The Druze students also rated stories with Arab content higher in interest value. In a similar study in Nigeria, Nigerian students learning and reading English as a second language had better literal reading comprehension when they read a culturally familiar story compared with students who read a culturally unfamiliar story. *Culturally familiar* was defined as stories with characters and situations that would be known to the students, such as traditional Nigerian tales.

An ethnographic (nonexperimental) U.S. study with low-achieving middle school Latino students found a number of possible benefits to using reading materials with culturally relevant topics (e.g., making tamales and other traditional family events). Quotes and observations of students suggested that the familiar materials led to students' becoming more interested in reading and being able to make more sense of what they were reading. Students were also able to use strategic reading procedures such as questioning, predicting, and relating to their own experiences since they could make more sense of the texts. For example, in reading a story about a meal involving friends and extended family, one student said it made him think of when some of his family first arrived and how in his family they prepare food that his uncle likes. Another student was able to relate a story about weeding a cornfield to his own experience in Mexico ("It makes me think of one day when we were weeding in the cornfield and there was an animal . . .").

Strictly speaking, the effect of the culturally familiar text per se is unknown in this study, since only culturally familiar text was used, and therefore we can't compare its effects with the effects of *non*culturally familiar text. In addition, the researcher used considerable amounts of Spanish with the students (the reading material and the language they conversed in), so it is quite possible that using the home language is what facilitated more engagement in reading and greater strategy use (see Chapter 2 on home language influences on reading achievement). Nonetheless, comments from the students, as illustrated above, indicated that they made connections with the text based on their own experiences, which were related to the content of what they read.

A very informative ethnographic case study reviewed by the NLP made a similar point about how familiar materials and experience can help promote literacy development among second-language learners. A researcher in England examined the literacy development of a Gujarati (from northwest India) child who attended a London multilingual and multicultural preschool where parents and children were invited to bring literacy materials from home in the home language. (This study is also relevant to the following section on parent and family influences and provides additional support for the use of the home language, as discussed in Chapter 2.) Home materials were placed in a "home corner" and a "writing area," and parents and children were invited to write in different languages and genres—cards, letters to relatives, posters, and travel brochures. The study nicely illustrates connections the children made between their areas of home experience and their classroom activities, particularly around literacy. The researcher found that letter writing at home, together with letter writing opportunities in preschool, probably contributed to the case study child's knowledge about writing letters and written conventions in both English and Gujarati. The mother reported that her daughter sat next to her at home, with pen and paper, saying "I am writing a letter" as the mother wrote letters to India. At preschool, the girl learned to write her name in English, and her mother showed her how to write it in Gujarati while providing additional opportunities for learning written Gujarati (this was observed directly by the researcher). When writing in the classroom, the child used Gujarati and English and demonstrated knowledge of appropriate form (e.g., writing in straight lines across the page) and content (e.g., news about the family's shop and family members).

Another study in England illustrated how a lack of cultural-background knowledge can be an obstacle for ELLs. Students from diverse linguistic backgrounds learning English as a second language performed more poorly than native English speakers on a reading test, even when it was administered orally. Test items required cultural-background knowledge that most of the ELL students did not have, for example:

Jimmy _____ tea, because he was our guest. Choices, with the correct answer italicized: (1) washed the dishes after, (2) was late for, (3) *got the best cake at*, (4) could not eat his.

Interestingly, the researchers found that on this particular item the ELL group performed equally as poorly as an English-only "working class" group, suggesting the required cultural knowledge might be related to social class (which, in fact, is another facet of culture, in this case perhaps middle-class English culture) and not necessarily ethnicity or national origin.

Finally, a similar study in the United States of Latino ELLs and monolingual English speakers found the same thing—lack of background knowledge led to poor test performance. This study went a step further and demonstrated that when ELLs had equivalent or greater background knowledge about specific test items, their performance and that of the monolingual English speakers was similar. The researcher wrote that "once prior-knowledge differences are taken into account, there is no longer any significant difference in passage performance between the two groups" (G. E. García, 1991, p. 381).

These studies make a reasonably compelling case that using or building on familiar material and experiences helps English learners as they read and acquire literacy skills in English. This suggests that when students are reading in a language they are learning, we must look for ways to help support the reading either by providing material with content that is already familiar or else teaching students sufficient content and background knowledge to permit comprehension of material they are given. The important point is that teachers must think about the relationship among the reader, the text, and knowledge that is required to make the text comprehensible. Teachers must think about this for all their students, but it is particularly important for students who are expected to learn content and a second language simultaneously.

These studies show the influence of background knowledge on reading comprehension, but a set of studies reviewed by the NLP also found that ELLs' proficiency in the language of the text had a much stronger influence on comprehension. In other words, reading familiar content helps comprehension, but knowing well the language in which the material is written helps comprehension even more. So while we can support ELLs' English reading comprehension and English literacy development more generally by providing materials with familiar content, promoting the development of their English language proficiency is probably an even more powerful way to support their English literacy achievement. (See Chapter 4 on promoting English language proficiency.)

## DOES *FAMILIAR* NECESSARILY MEAN *CULTURALLY FAMILIAR?*

It seems pretty clear from the studies described earlier that using familiar material and experiences can help support reading comprehension and, more generally, promote literacy development for second-language learners. One question raised by these studies, however, is what makes something familiar? Does *familiar* necessarily mean *culturally* familiar, as *culturally* is typically used? When we say that familiar materials help support ELLs' literacy, does that mean materials must be part of their ethnic or national-origin (e.g., Mexican, Cambodian) culture?

The answer is not necessarily. There are many ways that something can become familiar; the key is that it be part of an individual's *lived experience*. Certainly, culturally rooted practices such as celebrations, rituals, typical activities, and ways of interacting can be part of individuals' lived experiences—assuming they actually experience them! But people can have all sorts of other experiences that are not necessarily part of their natal cultures. Although students can come from isolated rural areas in their home countries, for example, they also become exposed to many sorts of media, interact with individuals from different sociocultural groups, see posters and billboards, learn at school and on the job, and so on. These experiences can all lead to greater familiarity with a range of topics that go beyond what people know from experiences solely in their own cultures. Educators should obviously not assume students from different sociocultural groups are only familiar with what is rooted in their natal cultures.

The studies described earlier provide several good illustrations. For example, the case study of the Gujarati girl in the multilingual and multicultural preschool revealed many examples of building on experiences and materials that were familiar to the children although not part of their home cultures. The preschool successfully used these experiences and materials as a basis for promoting children's literacy development. The mother of one child reported that he loved to watch cooking programs on television and could relate how to prepare a dish he had just seen demonstrated. In the classroom, the researcher reports that this child "produced a recipe involving 'one apple, two oranges, and a cake with jelly.'" Other children used a *Lion King* poster (produced by one of the parents in Spanish) to write out "El Rey León." Another child wrote out and built a dramatic play routine around lottery tickets. In other words, the connections children made were with their lived experiences rather than elements of their ethnic culture. They were encouraged by the preschool to build on familiar topics, themes, and texts that were part of the world around them. The researcher provides compelling evidence that children drew on these resources to engage in literacy activities and develop literacy skills in their first and second languages.

Another compelling example is provided by the study of Latino ELLs and monolingual English speakers by G. E. García (1991). In that study, students took a reading test made up of six short passages on different topics followed by comprehension questions about each passage. The researcher administered orally a test of students' knowledge about each topic. The ELL students knew less than the monolingual English speakers on four of the six topics and, accordingly, did more poorly on the corresponding comprehension questions. However, the Latino students knew at least as much as the English speakers about two of the topics—piñatas and polar bears—and their comprehension scores on these two passages were similar to those of the English speakers. Piñatas are stereotypically Mexican, so it is no surprise that the Latino students had the background knowledge. The author does not explain how it happened that the children knew about polar bears, however. It is possible children had recently studied them in school. Regardless, the point is that when the Latino and English-only children had the same degree of background knowledge, their reading comprehension scores were nearly identical. This was true whether the topic was piñatas or polar bears.

The scenario in Box 7.1 relates instruction to material that is somewhat familiar and meaningful to the students (their own family history) and includes family members in the lesson. Additionally, the teacher provides background knowledge so the concept of immigration is familiar to the students.

## Box 7.1

### Sociocultural Scenario

Mrs. C. is teaching a fifth-grade social studies lesson on immigration. Before reading the textbook chapter, she begins by showing pictures of her family members who were immigrants. She then puts on a babushka (scarf) and

*(Continued)*

(Continued)

a long skirt, and she becomes her own immigrant grandmother. Speaking in the first person, she tells the story of when, how, and why she came to America. As she tells her story, she holds up vocabulary cards with the words the class had previously gone over—*immigrant, motivation, perspective,* and *interview.* She uses each word in context. ("I am an immigrant from Russia. I used to live in Russia, but I came to live in America. My motivation or reason for coming to America was....Our perspective, or opinion, on leaving Russia was....") She then invites students to interview her (she uses this word purposefully) and ask her questions about her life.

Students are then told they will do an assignment in which they interview an immigrant they know. It can be a family member or, if that is not practical, a neighbor or a teacher. The students and Mrs. C. discuss possible interview questions. First as a class, then in small groups, students develop a series of questions they will ask in their interviews. Mrs. C. makes sure that all students ask questions about country of origin, motivation for coming to the United States, what they think about immigration to the United States, and what they miss most about their home country. Mrs. C. also makes sure students ask questions on topics that might be of particular interest to them. Students are given two days to complete the interview and return to class with written responses.

When they bring in their interviews two days later, students first share in small groups one or two responses they found most interesting. Then, in the whole class, Mrs. C. takes responses from about four students (some volunteers and some Mrs. C. calls on) and records them on a graphic organizer on the board, using headings based on the interview topics:

| Person Interviewed | Country of Origin | Motivation for Coming to the United States | Perspective on Leaving Home Country | Perspective on Coming to United States |
|---|---|---|---|---|
|  |  |  |  |  |
|  |  |  |  |  |
|  |  |  |  |  |
|  |  |  |  |  |

Mrs. C. then has students get back into their groups and fill out their own charts using information from each group member. The next day Mrs. C. will use the group's charts to discuss with the class the immigrant experience. For example, what motivates people to leave their homes? Why did they choose to immigrate to the United States? What is their perspective on immigrating? What sorts of things do they like about their new home? Dislike? What sorts of things do immigrants miss most? Is immigrating to a different country a good or bad idea? Why? What if you really don't have any choice?

## PARENTS AND FAMILIES

The role of parents and families in children's academic achievement has been a topic of research for the past half century. Studies have found that families play a very important role in their children's education, and they influence educational outcomes in many ways. The same is generally true for the families of ELLs. The NLP drew two conclusions about parents and families that are of particular interest to us here.[2]

One conclusion—which will surprise no one—is that home literacy experiences and opportunities seem to have an effect on ELL students' academic achievement. This conclusion comes from correlational studies, and readers should keep in mind what we discussed in Chapter 1 about this type of study (see discussion of correlation and causation in Chapter 1). Although we often interpret correlations as implying causation, in fact we can't be sure what causes what. Nonetheless, studies have generally found an association (or correlation) between literacy in the home and children's academic achievement, and it is at least plausible that one contributes to the other. Different studies have found correlations between the following:

- Number of books in the home and fourth-grade children's scores on an English reading comprehension test
- Kindergarten children's use of phonics worksheets sent by the teacher and children's early reading achievement (both in Spanish)
- How much time families of early elementary students spend together doing religious literacy activities and children's self-concept as readers
- English or Spanish literacy experiences in the home (e.g., reading, being read to, having books and other literacy materials) when

---

[2]A third conclusion was that the relationship between home language use and language-minority children's literacy outcomes in English is unclear. This issue will be discussed briefly at the end of the chapter when we address reading to children at home.

children were in kindergarten and English reading achievement in middle school

- The extent to which children's homes provided a stimulating learning environment and adolescent students' school and functional literacy

Findings are not totally consistent, however. Two studies found no correlation between time parents spend reading in the home and children's reading achievement. Another study found that parents' reading of booklets with short stories sent by the classroom teacher was not correlated with children's achievement. Nonetheless, there was a fairly clear pattern suggesting what most teachers already suspect: More literacy activity at home predicts higher levels of achievement for ELL students.

The second conclusion about parents and families is especially pertinent to the goals of this book and particularly important for educators to heed. The NLP concluded that parents of English learners are willing and generally able to help their children succeed academically, but that schools "underestimate parents' interest, motivation, and potential contributions . . . [and therefore] do not take full advantage of home resources that could help enhance outcomes for children" (August & Shanahan, 2006, p. 314 ).

The NLP reviewed several studies suggesting that the parents of ELLs are deeply interested in and concerned about their children's school achievement, primarily because they see education—or more precisely, formal schooling—as key to economic and social mobility for their children. Given an opportunity, parents could make a difference in their children's school success; however, they often lack the knowledge or the confidence about what they can actually do to help. Despite generally low levels of formal education themselves, as well as difficult circumstances ranging from very low incomes to precarious immigration status to lack of English proficiency, studies have concluded that parents of ELL students want to help their children succeed in school and can do so, but educators typically underestimate the role parents can play.

One ethnographic study in England showed that the parents of an English-speaking child and the parents of a Bengali-speaking English learner were equally interested and motivated to support their children's school success, but the Bengali mother lacked knowledge of how the school system worked and the unspoken expectations about communicating with teachers. Because of little communication originating from the home, the teacher assumed that Rahman (who was in a group of lower-achieving children) got "no support from home" (Brooker, 2002, p. 305), an assumption flatly contradicted by interviews and observations in the child's home. In contrast, the mother of the English-speaking child knew the system and the importance of regular communication with the teacher, which led to her son's being placed in a higher-achievement group and generally enjoying superior learning opportunities.

A U.S. study reported similar findings. The parents of low-income Latino students highly valued their children's school success and in some cases were able to support it directly. But generally, teachers assumed parents were uninterested or else so economically stressed that they did not have the time or energy to be concerned with school achievement. The assumption was simply incorrect.

Several other studies reviewed by the NLP reported school success stories—cases of schools with large ELL enrollments where student achievement was high—and one of the plausible explanatory factors was home and parent involvement in children's academics. In one of these studies, Spanish reading achievement in a predominantly Hispanic elementary school went from about the 30th to the 60th national percentile over a two- to three-year period. One of the changes at the school involved increased parent and home involvement in children's beginning literacy development. Whereas in previous years no systematic attempts had been made to involve parents in helping their children learn to read, teachers began sending home books and other reading materials, including homework and other assignments designed to promote literacy.

Another study documented a successful and relatively high-achieving school (this time achievement was measured in English). Not only was average achievement relatively high but there were also minimal achievement discrepancies between English speakers and English learners at the school. Among the explanatory factors revealed by the authors was ongoing contact and communication between the school and community. Overwhelming majorities of parents and teachers felt there were good home-school relations. Volunteers from the community worked directly with the children and helped teachers develop classroom materials. The study's authors report that the school's staff tried to improve the home-school connections even further by improving the quality of homework teachers assigned.

In neither of these two studies can we say conclusively whether parent involvement was the critical factor explaining the schools' success. Authors of both readily acknowledge that many other factors were in play at each school. As we discussed in Chapter 1, there were many confounding variables, that is, other influences besides parent involvement that could explain—fully or in part—the improvements in achievement. Nonetheless, both studies reinforce the point that parents are valuable potential allies who could help their ELL children improve school achievement.

One important issue that surfaces regularly is what language parents of ELLs should be encouraged to use with their children at home. Unlike language of instruction at school, for which we have numerous studies, many of them experimental (see Chapter 2), we have far fewer studies, and almost no experiments, on language use at home. The issues and how proponents of contrasting positions line up are analogous: On the one hand, some argue that more English at home, even if parents are limited in their

English proficiency, will promote greater English proficiency for children. On the other, some argue that parents should use their stronger language with children, which will then provide a more solid linguistic and cognitive foundation for their academic development. The NLP found that the research in this area is too equivocal to reach firm conclusions. However, specifically with respect to early literacy development, we do have a small cluster of experimental studies pointing to the benefits of parents using the home language in their literacy interactions with children.

Hancock (2002) studied the effects of kindergarten children taking home books in either English or Spanish to read with their parents. Results indicated that providing reading materials *in Spanish* led to more enhanced preliteracy skills (e.g., concepts of print) *in English* than did providing English reading materials for children to take home. Consistent with Hancock's findings, Koskinen, Blum, Bisson, Phillips, Creamer, and Baker (2000) found that sending home and promoting the use of books and tapes *in English* had *no effect* on first-grade ELLs' literacy development *in English*. More recently, Roberts (2008) reports two experiments involving Spanish- and Hmong-speaking children. Roberts compared the effects of sending home storybooks in English or a child's home language on children's acquisition of storybook vocabulary in English. In the first study, children who received the home-language storybooks learned more storybook vocabulary, as measured in English; in the second study there were no differences.

We should bear in mind that these studies did not manipulate the language generally used by parents and children in the home. Such an intervention, admittedly, would be difficult to implement and study. Nonetheless, the much more circumscribed manipulations suggest that, at least among young ELLs, enhancing home literacy experiences in the first language might have more positive effects on early literacy development than attempting to enhance home literacy experiences in English.

More generally, the challenge is for educators to find ways to connect with parents to communicate with them what they can do to support their children's school achievement. There is potentially a wide range of ways to accomplish this, from helping children learn basic skills and applying them outside of school (which is more plausible when children are in the earlier grades) to making sure children attend school and arrive prepared. The key is probably communication; studies have shown that the parents of ELLs are simply not sufficiently informed of what they can do to help ensure their children are successful in school. By bridging this communication gap, educators are likely to find willing (and grateful) allies.

## RECOMMENDATIONS

- **Use reading and other instructional materials with some degree of familiarity to ELLs**. The content of these materials can come from the students' home cultures and from what is familiar to students in their other out-of-school experiences (pop culture, media, trips, and other experiences). *However, teachers must teach ELLs academic subject matter that is essential for school success, which will necessarily include materials and content with which students are not yet familiar.* For instruction to be meaningful, teachers must keep in mind the relationship among the reader, the text, and knowledge needed to make the text comprehensible. Look for ways to help support reading comprehension by teaching students sufficient content and background knowledge to permit comprehension of material they are given.

- **Using behavioral or interactional styles to which students are accustomed might promote student motivation and engagement.** Teachers might consider observing closely how students interact among each other and with their parents. Although teachers are neither peers nor parents, and cannot interact with students as their peers and parents do, teachers might "act as anthropologists" and learn about students' behavioral patterns. This might provide ideas for how to interact with students and help prevent misinterpretations of students' behavior.

- **Find ways to involve parents in supporting their children's education.** Parents of ELLs highly value formal education and want their children to succeed in school. Virtually all parents can play an active supportive role, from helping with specific learning tasks (especially among younger children) to making sure students attend school prepared. The key is communicating with parents and working with them to see what they can do to support children's school success.

- **Consider making home visits to get to know parents, families, and the community.** This is a tall order, given the many obligations and pressures facing educators. In addition, some educators might not feel comfortable in unfamiliar neighborhoods where some of their students live. But if at all possible, this is an excellent way to learn about students' lives and let parents know you are interested in communicating with them about their sons and daughters to promote their school success.

# REFERENCES

ASCD Advisory Panel on Improving Student Achievement. (1995). Barriers to good instruction. In R. Cole (Ed.), *Educating everybody's children: Diverse teaching strategies for diverse learners* (pp. 9–20). Alexandria, VA: Association for Supervision and Curriculum Development.

Au, K., & Mason, J. (1981). Social organizational factors in learning to read: The balance of rights hypothesis. *Reading Research Quarterly, 17,* 115–152.

August, D., & Shanahan, T. (Eds.). (2006). *Developing literacy in second-language learners: Report of the National Literacy Panel on language-minority children and youth.* Mahwah, NJ: Lawrence Erlbaum.

Brooker, L. (2002). "Five on the first of December!" What can we learn from case studies of early childhood literacy? *Journal of Early Childhood Literacy, 2*(3), 292–313.

Carter, T., & Segura, R. (1979). *Mexican Americans in school: A decade of change.* New York: College Entrance Examination Board.

Cole, R. (Ed.). (1995). *Educating everybody's children: Diverse teaching strategies for diverse learners.* Alexandria, VA: Association for Supervision and Curriculum Development.

Durán, R. (1983). *Hispanics' education and background.* New York: College Entrance Examination Board.

Forman, E., Minick, N., & Stone, C. (1993). *Contexts for learning: Sociocultural dynamics in children's development.* Oxford, UK: Oxford University Press.

García, E. (1994). *Understanding and meeting the challenge of student cultural diversity.* Boston: Houghton Mifflin.

García, G. E. (1991). Factors influencing the English reading test performance of Spanish-speaking Hispanic children. *Reading Research Quarterly, 26,* 371–392.

Goldenberg, C., & Gallimore, R. (1995). Immigrant Latino parents' values and beliefs about their children's education: Continuities and discontinuities across cultures and generations. In P. R. Pintrich & M. Maehr (Eds.), *Advances in motivation and achievement: Culture, ethnicity, and motivation* (Vol. 9; pp. 183–228). Greenwich, CT: JAI Press.

Hancock, D. R. (2002). The effects of native language books on the pre-literacy skill development of language minority kindergartners. *Journal of Research in Childhood Education, 17,* 62–68.

Ima, K., & Rumbaut, R. G. (1989). Southeast Asian refugees in American schools: A comparison of fluent-English-proficient and limited-English-proficient students. *Topics in Language Disorders, 9,* 54–75.

Jacob, E., & Jordan, C. (Eds.). (1987). Explaining the school performance of minority students [Theme issue]. *Anthropology and Education Quarterly, 18*(4).

Koskinen, P. S., Blum, I. H., Bisson, S. A., Phillips, S. M., Creamer, T. S., & Baker, T. K. (2000). Book access, shared reading, and audio models: The effects of supporting the literacy learning of linguistically diverse students in school and at home. *Journal of Educational Psychology, 92,* 23–36.

McCarty, T. L., Wallace, S., Lynch, R. H., & Benally, A. (1991). Classroom inquiry and Navajo learning styles: A call for reassessment. *Anthropology and Education Quarterly, 22*(1), 42–59.

National Center for Education Statistics. (1992). *Language characteristics and academic achievement: A look at Asian and Hispanic eighth graders in NELS:88* (NCES 92–479). Washington, DC: U.S. Department of Education.

Roberts, T. (2008). Home storybook reading in primary or second language with preschool children: Evidence of equal effectiveness for second-language vocabulary acquisition. *Reading Research Quarterly, 43,* 103–130.

Rueda, R., August, D., & Goldenberg, C. (2006). The sociocultural context in which children acquire literacy. In D. August & T. Shanahan (Eds.), *Developing literacy in second-language learners: Report of the National Literacy Panel on language-minority children and youth* (pp. 319–339). Mahwah, NJ: Lawrence Erlbaum.

Saravia-Shore, M., & García, E. (1995). Diverse teaching strategies for diverse learners. In R. Cole (Ed.), *Educating everybody's children: Diverse strategies for diverse learners* (pp. 47–74). Alexandria, VA: Association for Supervision and Curriculum Development.

Sirin, S. (2005). Socioeconomic status and academic achievement: A meta-analytic review of research. *Review of Educational Research, 75,* 417–453.

Sue, S., & Padilla, A. (1986). Ethnic minority issues in the United States: Challenges for the educational system. In California State Department of Education, *Beyond language: Social and cultural factors in schooling language minority students* (pp. 35–72). Los Angeles: Evaluation, Dissemination and Assessment Center, California State University, Los Angeles.

Tharp, R. (1989). Psychocultural variables and constants: Effects on teaching and learning in schools. *American Psychologist, 44,* 349–359.

# 8

## *The Research Goes to School*

In the opening of this book we said that our goal was to make transparent for educators, policy makers, and interested readers what the research says—and what it *doesn't* say—about promoting academic success among ELLs. This is a confusing, difficult, and ideologically charged area—all the more reason that educators need to have a better basis than they generally do for making decisions about programs and policies for English learners. Not that this will take care of all the challenges these students and their teachers face. But we think it would help, if for no other reason than educators would be more informed and skeptical about some of the claims made about how to improve the achievement of this large and growing segment of our school-age population.

In this final chapter, instead of summarizing findings and recommendations—which we could do simply by assembling all of the recommendations in the preceding chapters—we instead attempt to synthesize the book's contents by presenting a series of scenarios. These scenarios illustrate and integrate what schools would look like if we put into practice the recommendations derived from the research we have reviewed and discussed. Much of the content of these scenarios will seem familiar since portions (or versions of them) were also presented in chapters throughout the book.

At the risk of being repetitious, we bring them together here, in one place, to try to illustrate the many interconnected factors that must be considered in creating effective programs for English learners. We recommend first skimming the complete text of each vignette (lefthand column) and returning to the commentary (righthand column) for a more careful reading. The commentary connects the scenario to the recommendations in the various chapters.

Readers will notice that the scenarios are heavily weighted toward elementary school. This is because there is far more research at the elementary level than the secondary. Therefore our claims about what is effective or "research-based" at the secondary level must be even more modest than those regarding the elementary level.

## ENGLISH LANGUAGE INSTRUCTION SCENARIOS

The first four scenarios depict lessons conducted in English. Following these four, we present two primary-language scenarios. Many elements of effective generic instruction will be evident but so will instructional adjustments geared toward helping ELLs become more successful in an all-English (or essentially all-English) academic environment. Certainly there are many other scenarios possible, but we present four, one each for reading/language arts and English language development and two for academic instruction—one at the elementary and one at the secondary level. These scenarios also depict the larger school context that must support and make possible effective practices in the classroom.

### Early English Literacy

Mr. G. teaches first grade at Buena Vista Elementary School, which is collaborating with two state-university faculty members on a grant focused on promoting early literacy development among English learners. The purpose of the project is to develop a coaching model that will help consultants and teachers work together to improve early literacy attainment for ELLs.

*Ongoing professional development (provided from within school staffs or by outside trainers) is focused on helping teachers achieve the learning goals for students. Ch. 6*

*Professional development here is ongoing and consists of (1) presentations and meetings with teachers and*

The university researchers have some ideas and protocols developed, but they want to work with teachers to pilot the protocols and get feedback from teachers about whether they believe the protocols will help improve instruction. The researchers will make changes in the protocols as they are piloted and teachers provide feedback. Researchers and their graduate students will also track achievement at the school, comparing it to past years and to that of other comparable schools in the district.

The teachers first attended a half-day session where the university faculty explained the goals of the project and solicited the participation of the K–2 teachers. Following the half-day kickoff, teachers began to attend monthly training sessions conducted by the university faculty; they were also observed once a month by the researcher/consultant. There are pre-coaching and postcoaching conferences before and after the observations.

In between trainings, teachers meet in grade-level teams to work on agreed-upon goals for student learning. The principal makes sure these meetings are regular weekly events by hiring two experienced aides to take each grade level for PE so that teachers are free to meet during this time. The principal makes clear his expectation that teachers are to focus on specific instructional issues at these meetings.

Teachers and researchers together identified specific learning goals for students. First-grade teachers had two areas of concern. One was the difficulty students were having in developing adequate word recognition skills; another was the development of content knowledge and vocabulary.

Teachers plan and then try out lessons based on what they are learning in their

*providers, (2) classroom practice coupled with coaching and feedback, and (3) teacher learning communities where teachers can work on and discuss ongoing challenges, issues, and successes with colleagues. There are collaborations with university researchers.*

*Professional development is supported by routine and systematic collaboration among teachers focused on achieving specific academic goals with students. Ch. 6*

*A culture of high expectations and accountability at all levels is supported by tangible steps to help teachers accomplish instructional goals for students. Ch. 6*

*Here the principal provides support for coherence from class to class with tangible steps to achieve learning goals.*

*Clear and challenging academic goals for students are explicitly articulated and understood by all teachers and embedded in well-structured curriculum. Ch. 6*

*A culture of high expectations and accountability at all levels is supported* monthly trainings. Lessons are structured, explicit, contain a clear objective, and provide ample opportunities for student practice. They track student progress using formative assessments, systematic teacher observation, and collection of student work. Teachers bring student work to the following week's meeting to discuss each lesson's success.

When the lessons are successful, teachers discuss what they think made the lesson successful; when the lesson is less successful, teachers analyze what happened and how to improve the lesson to get desired student outcomes. Through this process, the school is building capacity so that teachers will eventually coach one another.

Mr. G. is teaching a phonics lesson on the *ea* sound to his 20 first-grade students prior to reading an anthology story about going to the beach. Most are English learners whose primary language is Spanish; there are a few Vietnamese students as well. They are mostly at early intermediate English proficiency levels based on the state ELD assessment.

Mr. G. shows a picture of children playing in the sand at the beach and asks them to identify the beach and the sea in the picture.

He tells the students that today they are going to be learning to read words that have the long *e* sound that they hear in *beach* and *sea* and then are going to listen to a story about going to the beach.

But first he says, "Let's review the other way we learned to make the long *e* sound. Tell your partner another way we learned

*by tangible steps to help teachers accomplish instructional goals for students. Ch. 6*

*The foundation of an effective English literacy program for ELLs is similar to that of an effective literacy program for English speakers. Ch. 3*

*Use instructional modifications to help English learners acquire literacy skills in English. Ch. 3*

*Here Mr. G. uses visuals to introduce vocabulary.*

*Teach ELLs literacy skills explicitly. Ch. 3*

*Mr. G. clearly states the objective and lets students know explicitly what they will learn.*

*In addition to explicit skills instruction, use interactive teaching with ELLs, where teachers challenge* to spell long *e*." He gives students about a minute as he walks around and listens to gauge what they remember. Mr. G. then makes a web with *ee* in the center and lines going outward, like wheel spokes. He asks students to think of words with *ee*. After giving them about 10 seconds to think, he calls for volunteers. Students then offer *sleep, bee, keep,* etc.

Mr. G. goes on: "OK, the new way to write the long *e* sound is *ea*." Mr. G. points out that in Spanish this is the same sound that is made by the letter *i* or the word *y* (*and*). Mr. G. has the students practice saying single syllable, medial long *e* words, pronouncing the vowel as if they were saying *y* (*and*) in Spanish.

He shows the students the long *e* (*eagle*) card used by the school's reading program and explains that they are learning words where the *ea* is pronounced as a long *e*. As he writes each *ea* word on the board, the students use a blending routine. *S-ea…sea,* b-ea-ch…*beach,* b-ea-d…*bead.* Mr. G. shows a picture of the sea, the beach, and a necklace bead. The teacher models blending several words, and students repeat after him.

After blending each word on the board, Mr. G. tells the students, "Tell your partner how to spell the word _____." Mr. G. also asks the students to tell their partner a sentence with each word that has the *ea* sound.

Using flashcards and making sure everyone has an opportunity to participate, Mr. G. has the students read words they had already learned plus the new *ea* words he has introduced. He has them try to read fluently and quickly. He models blending for them, saying, "Listen as I do it. I read it like I'm talking—sea, beach. Make it sound like you're talking."

*students cognitively and linguistically. Ch. 3*

*Mr. G. provides opportunity for students to interact and use language.*

*Use instructional modifications to help English learners acquire literacy skills in English. Ch. 3*

*Mr. G. uses pictorial and textual clues and demonstrates blending on the board. Modifications are probably least necessary for phonics instruction, but Mr. G. still points out linguistic similarities and differences between L1 and L2.*

*Teach ELLs literacy skills explicitly. Ch. 3*

*Here Mr. G. provides multiple examples and repeated opportunities for practice in saying and reading the target words.*

*In addition to explicit skills instruction, use interactive teaching with ELLs, where teachers challenge students cognitively and linguistically. Ch. 3*

*Students interact periodically to process the information and practice reciting complete sentences with fluency.*

Mr. G. checks for understanding by whipping around the room and having each student read an *ea* word as he points to it. He asks, "What is the word? What vowel sound do you hear? What vowel team makes that sound?" It is repetitious, but it moves quickly and takes less than a minute for each child to respond individually.

Once he is confident that students have learned the new vowel digraph, he then turns to a story in the decodable text that reinforces the phonics rule he just taught. When it is time to read the story, he has the students do a "whisper read" individually first, before the group reads the story chorally.

Mr. G. calls up students individually during independent work time to read to him from the same decodable text. He notes on an index card any *ea* words read incorrectly. He will do a review and reteach the lesson with these students in the afternoon.

After finishing with the phonics portion of the lesson, Mr. G. has the class gather on the rug to begin the vocabulary portion of the lesson, before reading aloud a story about the beach. Mr. G. has already decided on seven vocabulary words he wants the students to know: *beach, castle, tunnel, sea, dig, build,* and *sand.* To tap prior knowledge and generate vocabulary, he asks the students if they have ever been to the beach and to name some things they might see at the beach. If they haven't been to the beach, he asks them if they have ever seen a movie about the beach or the sea (such as *Finding Nemo* or *The Little Mermaid*). He also shows several pictures of the beach and the sea to build background knowledge.

Mr. G. writes on a chart, "Things I can see at the beach!" Using the pictures and

*Effective teaching for ELLs is similar in many ways to effective teaching for English speakers. Ch. 5*

*As do all learners, ELLs benefit from clear goals and objectives, well-structured tasks, and adequate practice. Here, the teacher checks for understanding with each student.*

***Use instructional modifications to help English learners acquire literacy skills in English. Ch. 3***

*Mr. G. uses a variety of strategies to make content accessible. He taps prior knowledge, relates to personal experience, uses visuals to build background knowledge and introduce new vocabulary, and previews the pictures in the text to introduce additional vocabulary.*

their prior knowledge as support, students name things they might see at the beach as the teacher records the words on the chart. Next, Mr. G. does a "picture walk" with the book, asking the students what they see in the pictures; students offer new additions to the word chart. Mr. G. points out the identified target words in the pictures if the students have not offered these words. Mr. G. has also brought in a small jar of sand for the students to pass around and touch.

Mr. G. has sentence strips on the board that say, "What is this?" and "This is (a/an) _____." He asks the students to listen while he asks, "What is this?" and answers his own question. "This is sand," he says. He then asks the students, "What is this?" He holds up his hand as a wait signal, waits five seconds, and then signals the students to answer in unison, "This is sand." For the verbs, he asks, "What is he doing?" and models the response, "He is digging." He proceeds this way with the other target vocabulary words.

Occasionally, for the students just entering the early intermediate stage, he uses cognates (along with pointing) to clarify. For example, "The children are building a castle, *un castillo,* and digging a tunnel, *un tunel,* in the sand," he says. He has the students role play building a castle and digging a tunnel. Because Mr. G. does not know Vietnamese, he cannot provide L1 support in Vietnamese. Strategies such as visuals, sentence frames, and role play provide support regardless of the primary language.

He asks students, based on the pictures and the vocabulary words, to tell their partners what they think the story will be about. First Mr. G. gives some examples of using the target vocabulary in sentences. He says, "I think they will swim in the sea.

*Use L1 support in all-English classes to preview, clarify, and explain. Ch. 2*

*Use instructional modifications to help English learners acquire literacy skills in English. Ch. 3*

*Mr. G. uses role play and primary language (cognates) to clarify vocabulary. The teacher chooses strategies based on students' language proficiency levels as well as on reading level needs.*

**In addition to explicit skills instruction, use interactive teaching with ELLs, where teachers challenge students cognitively and linguistically. Ch. 3**

*Student interactions encourage using complete sentences and increasingly*

I think they will build a castle in the sand."

For homework, Mr. G. passes out a sheet with the day's *ea* words. The *ea* words have been added to the list of other long *e* words that students had previously taken home to practice reading and "show off" to their parents and other family members. Mr. G. has found that using this cumulative word list has helped the students build reading fluency. In addition to reading the words, the students are to retell the story to someone in their family. There is a place for parents to sign at the bottom of the sheet indicating the student had read the words to them and retold the story. If students don't bring back their homework more than twice, Mr. G. calls their homes or makes home visits.

*more complex linguistic structures, based on student proficiency levels.*

***Find ways to involve parents in supporting their children's education. Ch. 7***

*Parents value being able to support their children's learning at school, and practice homework that helps students solidify their skills and develop fluency is a good way to accomplish this.*

***Consider making home visits to get to know parents, families, and the community. Ch. 7***

## Elementary English Language Development Instruction, Supported by School and District

Ms. B. is a fourth-grade teacher at Riverside Elementary School, where there is a continuous focus on benchmark assessment across the curriculum. The regular assessment routine at Riverside is somewhat more work for teachers, and some complain that they spend too much time assessing students. But the staff sees it as beneficial since it gives them a nearly real-time picture of how students in their class, at their grade level, and across the school, are doing on important learning outcomes. Data collection and monitoring are well organized and are catalysts for discussion among teachers, instructional specialists, and administrators.

*Ongoing, systematic assessment provides teachers with timely information on how students are progressing with academic goals; uniform accountability systems measure student outcomes in academic subjects and English language development. Ch. 6*

*A culture of high expectations and accountability at all levels is supported by tangible steps to help teachers accomplish instructional goals for students. Ch. 6*

The principal talks about data at staff meetings and provides time for regularly scheduled team meetings to discuss what the data mean for how students are progressing. Discussions about assessment data are always in the context of thinking about how students at the school are faring academically and what the staff— teachers as well as administrators—can do to boost achievement. Data are never used punitively nor arbitrarily. The faculty has come to respect the principal's honest and clear-eyed view of the challenges they face and his continual striving to support their teaching and students' learning.

Riverside School purchased a progress-monitoring assessment specifically designed for ELLs that assesses students' oral and written English proficiency levels. It is used by all teachers four times a year as a formative assessment so that they don't have to wait for the once-a-year state ELD assessment results (which come too late in the year to be of much use for instruction and grouping anyway). The Riverside staff is also very familiar with the state's English language development and curriculum standards for the different content areas, and they regularly refer to these in planning instruction and discussing student progress.

ELLs at Riverside receive approximately 45 minutes of dedicated ELD instruction daily. The focus is on listening and speaking, but teachers reinforce these oral language skills by working on English language literacy skills during language arts and content instruction throughout the day. Conversely, during ELD time, teachers try to work on language skills that are important to what students are learning in their content area instruction.

Four times a year, the principal, the ELL coach, and the teachers look at formative

*Effective, visible, engaged leadership articulates at every opportunity the importance of providing challenging and meaningful learning opportunities for students. Ch. 6*

*There is schoolwide support for coherence from grade to grade and class to class regarding the selection, sequencing, and delivery of instruction; accountability measures will be more useful if there is general buy-in among administrators and staff. Ch. 6*

*Make ELD instruction a priority from the moment students walk into school, regardless of whether students are in primary-language or English-only programs. Ch. 4*

*Provide daily oral English language instruction. Ch. 4*

*Emphasize academic language—not only conversational language. Ch. 4*

*Use a separate time block for ELD instruction. Ch. 4*

*Professional development is supported by routine and systematic*

and, to some extent, state assessment scores to identify professional development needs. For example, the fall formative assessments revealed that early advanced and even advanced ELDs in the upper grades were weak in general academic vocabulary (e.g., *analyze, abandon, suspicious*) and content-specific vocabulary (e.g., *society, climate, evolution*). They also had difficulty with some complex verb forms such as the subjunctive (e.g., "If I were the boy...") and modal verbs ("I would tell my parents").

In their grade levels, teachers discuss lessons to target needs identified by the assessments, teach the lessons, and bring back student work to discuss and analyze results with colleagues. They do this routinely, working systematically over time to improve student learning in identified areas. The formative assessments help them track progress.

Working in grade-level teams, teachers send students to other classes for ELD based on their proficiency levels. The teachers have weekly one-hour grade-level meetings focused on one topic, such as formative or state assessment scores, and they do some of their planning together. The teachers arrange for small-group instruction based on formative assessment results. They also look for where the skill is taught in the district-adopted ELD or reading programs.

Ms. B. has all five levels of proficiency in her regular class, but every day at a set time, the fourth-grade teachers exchange students so that the students are grouped by proficiency level for a designated ELD block. One class has beginning and early intermediate students, another class has intermediate students, and a third class has early advanced and advanced students. The fourth class has English-only

*collaboration among teachers focused on achieving specific academic goals with students. Ch. 6*

*Ongoing professional development... focuses on helping teachers achieve learning goals for students. Ch. 6*

*Group ELLs carefully. Ch. 4*

*Here ELLs are not in classrooms segregated by language proficiency levels. Rather, they are in heterogeneous classrooms and then grouped by language proficiency specifically during ELD instruction. Grouping and instruction are carefully tailored to students' language learning needs.*

*There is routine and systematic collaboration among teachers focused on achieving specific academic goals with students. Ch. 6*

*There is schoolwide support for coherence from grade to grade and class to class regarding the selection, sequencing, and delivery of instruction. Ch. 6*

*Use a separate time block for ELD instruction. Ch. 4*

*Provide daily oral English language instruction, perhaps 45 minutes per day. Ch. 4* students. This is occurring schoolwide, with each grade level settling on the time they will trade students for ELD.

There are 30 students in Ms. B.'s ELD class, all early advanced and advanced levels. Even though the students have been put into different ELD classes based on proficiency, the teacher further differentiates instruction by separating a small group within the class when they need additional instruction on a skill.

Ms. B. usually uses the district-adopted ELD program, but one day a week the school uses the district-adopted Character Education program for teaching ELD. The students talk about pictures showing problematic situations that may occur with peers in school and then offer alternative solutions to solve the problems.

Ms. B. uses this as an opportunity to directly teach the early advanced students the subjunctive and to use phrases containing *could* and *would*, since it fits nicely with one of the needs identified at the last formative assessment. However, the formative assessment has indicated that most of the advanced students are already using these verbs correctly in spoken responses. In today's class she will have the advanced ELD students write scenarios in which they use these verb forms.

Ms. B. has the students sitting at tables of four to five students. She shows a large poster-size picture with a group of three students apparently excluding a single student from their group. The group in the picture seems to be talking about the student sitting alone at another lunch table. The single student looks sad. Most, but not all, in the larger group are laughing.

The teacher asks the open-ended question, "What do you see in the picture? What is the problem?"

*Continue ELD instruction at least until students reach Level 4 (early advanced). Ch. 4*

*Explicitly teach ELLs elements of English (e.g., vocabulary, syntax, conventions). Ch. 4*

*Here the students are learning about conditional auxiliary verbs.*

*Group ELLs carefully. Ch. 4*

*Here ELLs are not in classrooms segregated by language proficiency levels. Rather, they are in heterogeneous classrooms and then grouped by language proficiency specifically during ELD instruction. Grouping and instruction are carefully tailored to students' language learning needs.*

*Cooperative group work should provide opportunities for structured practice, not just spontaneous conversation. Ch. 4*

*Here the teacher first provides the opportunity for open-ended interaction.*

She directs the students to talk at their tables while she circulates and listens in on the conversations. She calls on volunteers to report aloud and says they should respond in complete sentences such as "We see..." or "We think the problem is..." Students can be creative in their responses so long as they use complete sentences and what they say is consistent with what is in the picture. This part of the lesson does not challenge students' levels of proficiency so no further instruction is needed.

Ms. B. calls on four students to come up and form a tableau of the scene in the picture and act it out.

Ms. B. says, "Now, we're going to talk about problems and solutions and how to express those ideas in English." At this point the teacher breaks the class into two groups. The advanced group will be working independently while she works with the early advanced and the few advanced students who need review.

Ms. B. gives clear instructions to the independent advanced group, which she also records on the board. Students are asked to develop a short skit demonstrating alternative solutions they could take, ending with the one they would take. Students are then to write their scenario in narrative form using the words *could* and *would*. They are to evaluate various solutions they could take and justify the one solution they would choose.

The teacher then turns to the early intermediate students. She draws two boxes with an arrow leading from the first box to the second. The first box is labeled "The Problem." Ms. B. records some of the responses offered by the students in the first box.

The second box is labeled "Possible Solutions." The teacher asks, "What is a

*Provide ELLs with ample opportunities for authentic and functional use of English. Ch. 4*

*Sheltered techniques probably help make academic content accessible for English learners while helping promote English language development. Ch. 5*

*Here Ms. B. uses visuals and role play.*

*Effective teaching for ELLs is similar in many ways to effective teaching for English speakers. Ch. 5*

*Here she establishes clear goals, models correct responses, and provides multiple opportunities to practice the structures.*

*Explicitly teach ELLs elements of English (e.g., vocabulary, syntax, conventions). Ch. 4*

*Here the students are learning about the modal verbs* could *and* would.

good solution? What *could* the boy do?" She defines *could* as what is *possible* to do, not necessarily what they will do. Underneath the second box, she writes, "The girl(s) could _____." Ms. B. models, "The girl in the group who is not laughing could get up and sit with the lonely girl." She asks for several volunteers to offer other ideas for what the characters could do. The students are directed to discuss more alternative solutions in their groups, but this time they are all to report aloud using the word *could* in their responses.

"We think/agree the girl(s) could _____."

Ms. B. records these alternatives in the Possible Solutions box. Then Ms. B. asks the students to choose the best solution from the ones offered and say what they *would* do if they were in that situation. She defines "I would" sentences as what you would *probably* do *if* you were in that situation. She points out the difference between what you *would* do and what you *will* do. She asks, "What would you do?" She writes on the board and models, "If I were the _____, I would _____." She tells the class, "Usually you hear people say, 'If I *was* the boy' or 'If I *was* the girl.' But that's not how we say it in English. We say, 'If I *were.*'

"So talk at your table about which one your table thinks is the best solution. And I want you to use the phrase, 'If I were _____, I would _____' and tell your group why you would do that. Then we'll share with the class." The students again discuss in their groups, but this time they are all to report aloud using the sentence, "If I were _____, I would _____" in their response.

*Provide ELLs with ample opportunities for authentic and functional use of English. Ch. 4*

Returning to the original tableau, the students with Ms. B. create a skit acting out the various solutions.

After the lesson the teacher calls the group back together, and both groups perform their skits for the whole class. Near the end of class, the teacher gives the students "think time" to come up with one sentence on any topic, using either *could* or *would*. They each tell their sentence to a neighbor.

When class is over, the students' "ticket out the door" is to give the teacher their one sentence correctly using "If I were _____, I could_____," or "If I were_____, I would _____."

*Effective teaching for ELLs is similar in many ways to effective teaching for English speakers. Ch. 5*

*Here she continues to model, provides numerous opportunities for oral language practice, checks for understanding, and provides closure.*

## Elementary Academic Instruction, Supported by Connections With Student Sociocultural Backgrounds

Mrs. C. is teaching a fifth-grade social studies lesson on immigration. ELD levels range from early intermediate to fluent English.

She begins by showing pictures of her immigrant family members.

She then puts on a babushka (scarf) and a long skirt and becomes her own immigrant grandmother.

Speaking in the first person, she tells the story of when, how, and why she came to America. She points to Russia on a map.

As she tells her story, she holds up vocabulary cards with the words *immigrant, motivation, perspective, ancestor,* and *descendant,* using each word in context. ("I am an immigrant from Russia. I used to live in Russia, but I came to live in America. My motivation or reason for coming to America was . . . .")

*Sheltered techniques probably help make academic content accessible for English learners while helping promote English language development. Ch. 5*

*Mrs. C. uses photos, maps, and a replica costume to pique the students' interest in her portrayal of her grandmother.*

*Keep in mind the fundamental challenge ELLs in all-English instruction face: learning academic content while simultaneously becoming increasingly proficient in English. Ch. 5*

*Here students learn content-specific vocabulary like* immigrant, motivation, *and* perspective *taught in a meaningful context. Vocabulary is directly taught using vocabulary cards and a meaningful context.*

Students are then invited to interview her, that is, ask her questions in preparation for the interview they will conduct on their own.

Students are asked to interview an immigrant. It can be a family member or, if that is not practical, a neighbor or a teacher.

The students and Mrs. C. discuss possible interview questions and decide on the following:

- Where did you come from? When did you come?
- What are some things you remember about immigrating?
- What was your motivation for coming or leaving?
- What was your perspective, or how did you feel about immigrating?

Students return with their responses the next day. Responses are recorded on a cause-and-effect graphic organizer under person/country/motivation (or reason) for immigrating/perspective (or views) on immigrating.

The teacher models using sentences with *because*. She uses information recorded on the graphic organizer:

- My grandmother came to America because . . .
- My grandparents were sad about leaving Russia because . . .
- My grandparents like it in America because . . .

*Provide ELLs with ample opportunities for authentic and functional use of English. Ch. 4*

*Here students practice, in the form of interview questions before conducting the interviews, the English that the teacher modeled.*

*Find ways to involve parents in supporting their children's education. Ch. 7*

*The interviews allow for parent involvement in the assignment.*

*Use reading and other instructional materials with some degree of familiarity to ELLs. Ch. 7*

*The content of these materials is coming from the students' home cultures and what is familiar to them in their other out-of-school experiences.*

*Sheltered techniques probably help make academic content accessible for English learners while helping promote English language development. Ch. 5*

*The graphic organizer is such a technique and connects content with the language activity to follow.*

*Explicitly teach ELLs elements of English (e.g., vocabulary, syntax, conventions). Ch. 4*

*When teaching academic language, do not focus only on vocabulary; focus on syntax and text structures as well. Ch. 4*

*Effective teaching for ELLs is similar in many ways to effective teaching for English speakers. Ch. 5*

Students orally share their immigrant responses using similar sentences. Students then write their sentences using the information they collected. These become the basis for a story they will write.

*The teacher models before asking students to practice (guided and independent) using the vocabulary and the sentence structures.*

**Keep in mind the fundamental challenge ELLs in all-English instruction face: learning academic content while simultaneously becoming increasingly proficient in English. Ch. 5**

*In this case, there are both content and language goals: immigration and cause-and-effect sentences and asking questions. The lesson includes listening and speaking (the interview), reading (the text), and writing (sentences and the story).*

## High School Content Instruction (and Reading Expository Text)

Mr. P. is teaching a lesson to his psychology class titled "What Is Seeing?" The lesson is about sensation and perception. Mr. P. is teaching it to help students read and comprehend their psychology text. The book is informative but written at a fairly high academic level. Many of the students are struggling readers and approximately 40 percent are second-language learners at the intermediate proficiency level. Mr. P. reports that they are relatively fluent speakers of conversational English but have difficulty reading and comprehending academic text.

His objectives for today's class are that students will be able to do the following:

1. Define *sensation* and *perception*, particularly with respect to seeing

**Keep in mind the fundamental challenge ELLs in all-English instruction face: learning academic content while simultaneously becoming increasingly proficient in English. Ch. 5**

**Effective teaching for ELLs is similar in many ways to effective teaching for English speakers. Ch. 5**

objects, and explain the process of sensation and perception.

2. Apply knowledge of (a) word relationships, such as roots and affixes to derive meaning from literature and texts in content areas, and (b) cognates and false cognates to derive meaning from literature and texts in content areas. Use sequence words to explain the process of sensation and perception.

Mr. P. says, "OK, we're going to talk about seeing. What does it mean to see something? Think about it; don't yell out." He pauses a few seconds and then asks two or three students.

He then asks the students to read what he has written on the board:

rat eht saw tac ehT

"What do you see there?" he asks. He waits a few seconds and then calls on students. One says he sees a bunch of letters and two words. Another says he sees misspelled words. "What about a mixed-up sentence with jumbled-up words? Does anyone see that?" He points as he reads, "'The rat saw the cat.' Different people look at the same thing but can *see* different things," he says.

Next he cuts a square out of a piece of paper and holds it up. "What do you see now?" Students answer, "A square." "OK, now turn your head sideways like this," and he shows them what he means. "Now what do you see? Do you see the diamond?" He then cuts out a diamond and repeats the above, this time going from diamond to square. "Same shapes, right? But you can see different things."

"OK, one more," he says, and he holds up this diagram:

*Use L1 support in all-English classes to preview, clarify, and explain. Ch. 2*

*Sheltered techniques probably help make academic content accessible for English learners while helping promote English language development. Ch. 5*

*Effective teaching for ELLs is similar in many ways to effective teaching for English speakers. Ch. 5*

*Here the teacher piques interest through experiential and concrete activities to engage the students.*

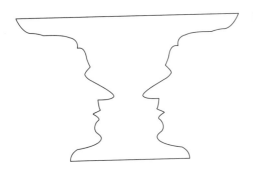

"What do you see now?" Most students say they see a cup. A couple of students say they see the two faces looking at each other. Those who saw the cups are startled to realize that the drawing does indeed look like two faces looking at each other.

Mr. P. says, "Notice how in each case [points to each as he says them: the jumbled words and sentence, the square or diamond, the cup or two faces], the information that came into your eyes [motions something coming into his eyes] did not change. What changed was what you thought it was [points to his head]. What comes into your eyes is sensation; what you think something is is perception."

"Today we're going to talk about how seeing requires *sensation* and *perception*," the teacher says as he writes the words on the board.

Mr. P. has written the definitions on sentence strips, which he tapes on the board next to the words he wrote.

"Today we are going to learn about how we see things. We receive or take in information from our environment—*sensation* [he points to *sensation*]—then we make it meaningful so we understand it—*perception* [he points to *perception*]. These involve two different processes; we will learn about both so you can see how we actually see things. Seeing things requires using not only our eyes but our brains.

*Teach academic language as a key part of content area instruction. Ch. 5*

Here the teacher explicitly teaches content-specific vocabulary.

*Effective teaching for ELLs is similar in many ways to effective teaching for English speakers. Ch. 5*

The teacher clearly states the lesson's goal and provides clear definitions of key vocabulary.

*Sheltered techniques are probably helpful in accomplishing the goal of making academic content accessible for English learners while promoting English language development. Ch. 5*

The teacher is using textual clues in the form of definitions on sentence strips.

"Our goal for this lesson is that you will be able to describe the process of how we are able to see by, first, taking in information with our eyes and then making sense of this information with our brains. If you can do this, it will help you read and understand the chapter in your psychology book.

"Let's take a closer look at the word *perception*." Mr. P. draws a circle on the board and in the center writes *"ceps: Latin for taker."* "It is like the Spanish word *percepción* [writes it on the board, on the left side of *ceps*, under a heading that says *"Español"*; he circles *cep*], which also comes from the same root. In English the word is *perception*." (Writes *perception* on the board, to the right of *ceps*, under a heading that says "English"; he circles *cep*.)

"Look at the definition on the sentence strip—how is perception (or being able to perceive) related to *ceps,* Latin for take?" He waits a few seconds to give students a chance to think about this question; a few students raise their hands and offer reasonable suggestions. Mr. P. goes on: *"Perceive* means to grasp or take with the mind." Mr. P. uses both hands to make an exaggerated grasping motion in front of him and brings both hands, fingers first outstretched and then closing in, toward his forehead to show "taking with the mind." *"Take* is like *receive* and even *receive* comes from the same root *ceps."* He writes *receive* on the board, under *perception,* and circles *ce.* "Another word from *ceps* is *receptor."* He writes *receptor* on the board, under *receive,* and circles *cep.*

"Think of when a soccer player kicks a pass or a football player throws a pass, and the other player receives it. We call that a reception, to receive the pass. We have receptors in the eyes that take in

*Use instructional modifications to help English learners acquire literacy skills in English. Ch. 3*

*Point out similarities (e.g., cognates) and differences (e.g., spelling patterns) between English and the primary language. Ch. 2*

Here the teacher uses primary-language support. He focuses on the similarities and differences between English and the primary language, using cognates and Latin root origins from which both the Spanish and English words are derived. He uses more familiar words also derived from these word origins.

*Sheltered techniques probably help make academic content accessible for English learners while helping promote English language development. Ch. 5*

Here the teacher relates the concept to personal experience and uses familiar concepts to clarify vocabulary.

*Use reading and other instructional materials with some degree of familiarity to ELLs. Ch. 7*

information from the outside. The brain then receives that information and gives it meaning."

Mr. P. makes a web around the circle with the words *reception, perception,* and *receptor,* which all derive from *ceps.* He then has students discuss other familiar words and their possible meanings, for example, *intercept, accept,* and *receptacle.*

Mr. P. continues, "Now let's look at how we *see* what is in our environment. First, we have to *sense* it, and that is done with our eyes." He shows a poster of a cross-section of an eye and points out the labeled parts and their functions. Students label the parts on a similar diagram as the teacher points out and discusses each one. "The pupil, lens, retina, and optic nerve are especially important for vision," Mr. P. says.

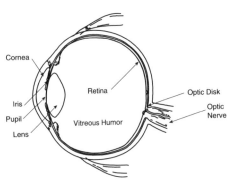

Mr. P. explains (pointing as he talks and making sure all students can see) how light waves bounce off objects (he holds an object to the left of the eye in the diagram and motions light hitting, bouncing off the object, and entering the eye) and enter the eye through the pupil. He continues, "The lens [points to the lens] focuses the light from the object onto the back of the eye [motions from lens to retina], where it hits the retina. The retina contains millions of receptors (remember *cept*—to take in [he points to it on the board]), which then take in the information

*The foundation of an effective English literacy program for ELLs is similar to that of an effective literacy program for English speakers. Ch. 3*

*Sheltered techniques probably help make academic content accessible for English learners while helping promote English language development. Ch. 5*

*Here Mr. P. uses illustrations. Students are engaged throughout as they record the information on their own diagram. The teacher gives clear input on the content objective.*

from the environment and send it to the optic nerve at the back of the eye. All of this is *sensation*. Taking in information from the environment, from what is out there." He motions all around to emphasize the environment.

The teacher goes on, "But then to see something, it's not enough only to sense it. Your brain also has to perceive it [points to *perceive* on the board]. Your brain has to take it [repeats motion with his hands in front of him, bringing both hands, fingers first outstretched and then closing in, toward his forehead to show 'taking with the mind']. So traveling through the optic nerve [points again to diagram], the image you see goes to the brain [points from the optic nerve to his head], where the brain organizes the information and gives it meaning. This is perception, and once you perceive it, you see it."

At this point Mr. P. has been providing a great deal of input and wants the students to discuss it a bit among themselves so he can hear if they are getting the concepts. So he tells the class, "OK, I've just given you a lot of information. I want you to think about what the difference is between what these two words [points to them] mean—*sensation* and *perception*. One is where information comes in from the environment; the other is where that information comes into your brain so you understand it. I want you to discuss with a person sitting next to you what each of these words means; give each other a little quiz to make sure you understand. Ask for examples to make sure you know them." Mr. P. then walks around the room, listening specifically for misconceptions and clarifying if he hears them.

Mr. P. then has the students preread the chapter they are about to read. In table groups, he has students discuss each of

*In addition to explicit skills instruction, use interactive teaching with ELLs, where teachers challenge students cognitively and linguistically. Ch. 3*

*Teach ELLs literacy skills explicitly. Ch. 3*

the photos, illustrations, charts, and graphs. He points out the focus question at the beginning of the chapter: What is the difference between sensation and perception? He points out each subheading and, based on the titles and photos, asks students to predict what they will learn about in each section (on each of the five senses with which we perceive the environment). Students then read the subheadings under the section of the chapter titled "Vision" with a partner.

One student reads a subheading section and the partner summarizes what he just heard. They alternate until the pages about "Vision" are read.

Students have a note-taking graphic organizer in the form of a flow chart to record what they learned so far about vision. Each box of the flow chart is numbered to indicate a step in the process. A list of previously learned sequence words is posted. Students are asked to label each box with the appropriate sequence word, such as *first, next, later, eventually,* and *finally.* Students record the process from sensory stimulus to visual perception. Students work with a partner, but each completes his or her own flow chart.

Each student fills in a chart using words and pictures that tell how we sense with our eyes and perceive with our brains.

Students are first asked to share the process of sensation and perception with their partner. Volunteers are then called upon to explain the process of how we see by using the words and pictures on the graphic organizer. Students are required to use the new vocabulary words (*sense* or *sensation; perceive* or *perception*) in the flow chart. The definition of *sensation* is to be in the opening sentence and that of *perception* in the closing sentence.

*Here the teacher uses comprehension strategies such as setting purposes for reading and prereading the text.*

**Teach ELLs literacy skills explicitly. Ch. 3**

**Sheltered techniques probably help make academic content accessible for English learners while helping promote English language development. Ch. 5**

*Here the teacher uses illustrated graphic organizers to organize information and make it manageable*

**Academic language instruction should include not only the vocabulary of the content subjects but the syntax and text structures as well. Ch. 4**

*In this case, the teacher is teaching the sequence text structure. Students are learning syntax as well as vocabulary.*

Students are then asked to describe the process in a written paragraph, using the graphic organizer as support. Here is an example:

> First, light hits an object, and the light waves bounce off at different wavelengths, or colors. Next, the light enters the eye. This is how we receive information from the environment (sensation). After the light enters the eye through the pupil, the lens focuses the image on the retina. The optical receptors in the retina then send the image to the optic nerve, and the optic nerve carries this information to the brain. Finally, the brain thinks about the sensory information received by the eye and organizes it. This gives the information meaning, which is perception. At this point, you see the object in the environment.

*The foundation of an effective English literacy program for ELLs is similar to that of an effective literacy program for English speakers. Ch. 3*

*Here students are asked to write a summary of what they have learned about how seeing requires both sensation and perception.*

## PRIMARY-LANGUAGE INSTRUCTION SCENARIOS

The final two scenarios depict programs where students receive primary-language instruction, that is, bilingual education.[1] These scenarios are pitched a little differently than the first four. Instead of focusing on a single lesson (within a schoolwide context), they describe a particular type of bilingual program.

Both scenarios are with Spanish-speaking ELLs. The reason for not including one of the more than 400 non-English languages spoken by students in U.S. schools is simply that students who are in primary-language programs in this country overwhelmingly come from Spanish-speaking backgrounds. Among the 346 two-way programs known to exist in the United States, 321 (93 percent) enroll Spanish-speaking students (http://www.cal.org/twi/directory/language.htm). Although there is no reason to believe that other language groups would not enjoy the same benefits of primary-language instruction that Spanish speakers do, the research for these other language groups is very sparse, if not missing altogether.

---

[1]We have relied on Genesee et al. (1999) for portions of the following scenarios.

The first scenario illustrates a transition program, where the primary language is used for reading and language arts (possibly for math and other content areas too) during the students' first two to three years of school.

The second of these scenarios illustrates two-way bilingual education (also known as dual language), where students from two different language backgrounds are in the same class, and the program's goal is bilingualism and biliteracy for all students. Readers might recall from Chapter 2 that the Center for Research on Education, Diversity and Excellence (CREDE) report concluded that long-term, sustained bilingual education aimed at promoting bilingualism and biliteracy produced superior outcomes compared to shorter-term programs, such as transitional bilingual education. In contrast, the National Literacy Panel (NLP) (and three other meta-analyses) concluded that the research does not permit informed judgments about the relative benefits of more versus fewer years of primary-language instruction. Despite this basic uncertainty, we include a two-way scenario because of the evident promise it holds. As we indicated in Chapter 2, this form of bilingual education helps ELLs maintain and develop home language skills and provides opportunities for children from different language backgrounds to become bilingual and biliterate. We believe these are important educational outcomes that benefit students, their communities, and society in general.

## Transitional Bilingual Education/Early Exit

Ms. L. is a fluent bilingual (Spanish and English) second-grade teacher at Las Palmas Elementary. Her students, now in the second half of second grade, are mostly intermediate English speakers; some are early advanced. All had entered kindergarten at the beginning and early intermediate English proficiency levels.

*If at all possible, teach students literacy skills in their home language. Ch. 2*

In Grades K–2, language arts and math instruction at the school are in Spanish. Science and social studies are taught in Spanish in kindergarten and the beginning of first grade; by the second half of first grade, teachers use sheltered instruction and content-based ESL to teach science and social studies concepts and English simultaneously. Students have art, music, and PE in English.

*Sheltered techniques probably help make academic content accessible for English learners while helping promote English language development. Ch. 5*

They receive at least 45 minutes per day of dedicated ELD instruction, geared to students' proficiency levels, from the time they enter the school.

Ms. L.'s language arts lessons are identical to grade-level language arts lessons anywhere, except that they are in Spanish. Actually, they are relatively more advanced than typical language arts lessons in second grade since children who learn to read in Spanish can learn more quickly (due to the simpler Spanish orthography) and therefore can read virtually any Spanish written text. Las Palmas's Spanish reading program is structured and explicit; most children master the skills of reading, and can read with considerable fluency, by Grade 2.

Because of the strong Spanish reading program, Ms. L. can have most children read a range of stories, chapter books, poems, and nonfiction works. She focuses on reading comprehension, vocabulary, writing, discussions, and book reports. She also has them read a lot of nonfiction, especially about topics she will cover in her sheltered social studies and science instruction. She finds that when the students become familiar with topics by reading and discussing them in Spanish, they do much better during English instruction on those same topics.

Students at Las Palmas typically transition to all-English instruction by the third grade. Students are generally at grade-level-appropriate reading and writing skills in Spanish and at least intermediate in their oral English proficiency.

Teachers get considerable help from parents, virtually all of whom can read and write in Spanish at least to some degree; many are fully literate in every

*Make ELD instruction a priority from the moment students walk into school, regardless of whether students are in primary-language or English-only programs. Ch. 4*

*Effective teaching for ELLs is similar in many ways to effective teaching for English speakers. Ch. 5*

*A culture of high expectations and accountability at all levels is supported by tangible steps to help teachers accomplish instructional goals for students. Ch. 6*

*Find ways to involve parents in supporting their children's education. Ch. 7*

respect. Practice homework is a regular feature of the program at Las Palmas, and all children routinely take home stories, worksheets, and books they are to read and practice at home. Parents are very pleased to see the progress their children make and to be participants in it.

As a second-grade teacher, Ms. L. begins teaching math in English during the latter half of the year by using sheltered-instruction strategies such as visuals, word labels, gestures, demonstrations, props, and manipulatives. Social studies, science, art, music, and PE are in sheltered English, although the need to shelter art, music, and PE gradually diminishes. All of Ms. L.'s instruction is guided by both content and language objectives.

ELD lessons in the spring begin to include simple reading and writing activities such as poems, songs, and chants related to topics being studied in other curricular areas. The focus is on academic English that will help children succeed in the core curriculum. In her lessons, Ms. L. emphasizes the similarities between English and Spanish. She consults the state's ELD standards and the district's ELD program to get ideas for appropriate language objectives.

*Sheltered techniques probably help make academic content accessible for English learners while helping promote English language development. Ch. 5*

*Emphasize academic language—not only conversational language. Ch. 4*

## Two-Way or Dual-Immersion Programs

Mr. F. and Ms. D. teach in a Spanish-English two-way bilingual program at Emory Avenue Elementary School. This means that Spanish-speaking children and English-speaking children go to school together; the goal of their program is bilingualism and biliteracy by the end of elementary school. Unlike transitional bilingual programs, Spanish-speaking children do not "transition out" of Spanish

*If possible, maintain primary-language instruction throughout elementary school or beyond, such as in two-way bilingual programs. Ch. 2*

*Dual-language programs almost certainly help develop literacy and academic skills in the primary language. They might also have positive effects on achievement in English and student*

instruction once they achieve some threshold of English proficiency. Instead they continue receiving literacy and other academic instruction in Spanish in order to further develop their skills.

An important goal of the program is for students to develop positive cross-cultural relationships and attitudes toward speakers of other languages. Cultural awareness and appreciation are reflected in classroom lessons and activities and decorations in the school. Art, music, literature, customs, and historical and contemporary personages from the Anglo and Latino American worlds are amply represented.

Mr. F. is a native English speaker, although his Spanish is quite good; he took Spanish in high school and college and has traveled to Mexico and other parts of Latin America. Ms. D. is from Nicaragua, where she went to middle school before moving to the United States. In the United States, she graduated from high school and attended a state university before obtaining her teaching credential. Throughout high school and college she took advanced Spanish language and literature classes, and histories of Latin America and Spain, so she is extremely literate in Spanish and knowledgeable about the history and culture of the Spanish-speaking world. Her English is also excellent, and she did very well in her high school and college classes.

Dual-language programs almost certainly help develop literacy and academic skills in the primary language. They might also have positive effects on achievement in English and student attitudes toward different languages and cultures.

Mr. F. and Ms. D. teach fourth grade, and their classrooms are next door to each other. Each one has a class that is equally

*attitudes toward different languages and cultures.*

*If at all possible, teach students literacy skills in their home language. Ch. 2* split between students from Spanish-speaking homes and students who are English-only speakers, mostly Anglos but also a few African Americans.

Emory uses a "50/50" dual-immersion model, meaning that children receive half of their instruction in English and half in Spanish. In the early grades, children learn to read and write in both languages. They learn science, PE, and art in English and social studies and music in Spanish. In later years, they switch and learn science, PE, and art in Spanish and social studies and music in English, so that over the years children receive instruction in both languages in all content areas. There is always a designated Spanish teacher and designated English teacher for each subject. Teachers work in two-person teams, sometimes supplemented by an art, music, or PE "specialist," and they exchange students during instructional periods. In the early grades, one teacher teaches beginning and early English reading to the English speakers in both classrooms while the partner teaches beginning and early Spanish reading to the Spanish speakers. Later in the day they switch and the English speakers get Spanish reading; the Spanish speakers get English reading. Most of the day is spent in mixed-language groups. For example, one teacher will teach science in English to half of her class and half of her partner's class (mixed English and Spanish group), while the partner teaches social studies to the rest of the children in Spanish; they switch on alternate days.

Teachers not only coordinate their teaching schedules, they also work and plan together to provide thematic linkages across the curriculum to strengthen the coherence of the program and enrich language (and content)

*Students can be taught literacy skills in English while they are learning literacy skills in their home language. Ch. 2*

*There is schoolwide support for coherence from grade to grade and class to class regarding the selection, sequencing, and delivery of instruction. Ch. 6* learning opportunities. This year, in fourth grade, Mr. F.'s and Ms. D.'s students are working on a year-long unit of study about their state's history, physical characteristics, society, and culture. Mr. F. teaches history and math in English; Ms. D. teaches science and art in Spanish. Reading and language arts continue to be taught in both languages (in English by Mr. F. and Spanish by Ms. D.). For history, Mr. F. uses lots of pictures, videos, and maps; they also go on a field trip to a local museum. He tailors expectations for written products to students' English language proficiencies, but he continually encourages ELLs to strive for greater complexity and sophistication in their writing and oral language.

Mr. F. uses books, pictures, and other materials that show the experiences of immigrants from diverse cultural and linguistic backgrounds who have come to the state. Words, customs, and folk tales of some of the immigrant groups are familiar to some of the students, but students also learn about cultural and linguistic groups with whom they are not familiar and who comprise an important part of the state's history and contemporary social fabric.

Math lessons use examples and applications that are relevant to understanding the state's history, society, and physical characteristics. For example, the class is learning to add large numbers (up to millions) so they can calculate the impact different demographic groups have had on the state's population. In geometry they are learning about perimeter and area, so they learn about the size of land parcels obtained by settlers and how the parcels diminished in size as more settlers arrived. Mr. F. also teaches them to represent quantitative trends graphically, so they construct tables and graphs showing changes in population,

*Sheltered techniques probably help make academic content accessible for English learners while helping promote English language development. Ch. 5*

*Use reading and other instructional materials with some degree of familiarity to ELLs.... However, teachers must teach ELLs academic subject matter that is essential for school success, which will necessarily include materials and content with which students are not yet familiar. Ch. 7*

automobiles, speakers of languages other than English, and other interesting aspects of how the state had changed over the past 100 years.

Mr. F.'s lessons are well planned and structured. In today's lesson about the history of different cultural and linguistic groups in the state, he begins with a brief statement about the lesson's objective: "Students will be able to name from three to five different cultural groups who began settling in the state over the past 150 years, say when they started to arrive, and name two or three customs or practices they brought with them."

He then has a brief discussion with students to see what they remember from yesterday's lesson about cultural groups (he asks them if they recall the Spanish word for culture—*cultura*). He had first introduced the concept of "cultural group," and he wanted to make sure to review briefly this relevant background knowledge. He had students, in pairs, name and talk about some of the cultural groups in the state, based on the lesson yesterday.

"So now," Mr. F. continues, "Let's learn about when these different groups started to arrive and what sorts of things they brought with them that have contributed to what our state is like today." To help students keep track of the information, he hands out a chart titled "When did they arrive? What did they bring?" The chart has three columns: cultural group, year members of the group started arriving, and customs or practices they brought. Mr. F. says that in the lesson today they're going to fill out this chart and then keep it with their unit materials so that they can refer to it later as they continue learning about the state's history, culture, and economy.

*Effective teaching for ELLs is similar in many ways to effective teaching for English speakers. Ch. 5*

*Mr. F.'s lesson is very well designed and delivered. He has a clear goal that he communicates to students, he connects the previous day's learning with today's, he uses techniques to promote active student participation and engagement, he uses a chart to help students keep track of and organize complex information, he monitors what students are doing, and he checks for their comprehension.*

Mr. F. puts up an overhead transparency with the chart and says that they'll do a cultural group together. Then students will work in pairs to fill out information about additional cultural groups. He hands out an information sheet with pictures and other illustrations about the history of the African American population in the state, and he tells students to first read the information sheet silently to themselves, paying particular attention to information the chart asks for. "What information is the chart asking for?" he asks. "Don't call it out; think about it for a minute and then tell your partner." He says not to worry if they don't understand everything on the sheet; they should just try to get as much as they can.

After the students read silently for a few minutes, Mr. F. will read the sheet aloud, but first he says that when he gets to something in the text that provides information the chart asks for, students should raise their hands to signal it. They will then stop, underline the information on the sheet, and note it on the chart. Mr. F. then reads the sheet as students look and listen for relevant information. By the time he gets to the end of the information sheet, the columns are filled out for African Americans.

Mr. F. tells the class that he has information sheets for five other cultural groups and that they are to work in pairs to fill out the charts, just as he had done. But since he notices that some of the students are still not 100 percent sure what to do, he says that he is going to work through one other example. Those who want to follow along with him can do so; those who feel they can do it independently can do that.

By the end of the hour, most students have filled out the chart for four of the six groups, although some students have empty cells on the chart. Mr. F. says that they'll finish tomorrow and then play a game like Jeopardy, where they have to use what they are learning about these cultural groups.

When Ms. D. teaches the students science (in Spanish), she uses the same principles of effective instruction that Mr. F. does, except that she teaches in Spanish. Just as Mr. F. has to make adjustments for the English learners, Ms. D. has to make adjustments to make the content comprehensible to the Spanish learners. Ms. D.'s students learn about and create models of the state's ecosystems. They also learn about the different rocks and minerals found in the state and conduct experiments to compare their different physical properties, such as density and hardness. Working in cooperative groups, students make displays of the major land formations in the state. During art, Ms. D. shows them landscape paintings of famous painters, and students learn how to draw landscapes to serve as backdrops for their displays. During reading and language arts, students read (in both Spanish and English) short stories, poems, essays, and one or two chapter books by authors native to the state or about topics related to what they are studying. The two classes cover a lot of territory and many concepts.

*Teaching ELLs subject matter content in their primary language might be beneficial since it is probably a more efficient way to promote content knowledge than teaching content in a language students do not understand well. Ch. 2*

# 9

## Conclusion

### What's Next?

A s we indicated at the outset, this is not a methods book, nor is it a policy manual. We hesitate to make broad and glib statements about what our different audiences—teachers, administrators, and policy makers—"ought" to do. Yet we feel we should close with some indication of how we think we should proceed if we are to deal seriously with the issues we have addressed in this book. The suggestions that follow are meant to provide the broad contours of a framework within which educators and policy makers can create effective programs for ELLs.

An important principle applicable across the board is that anyone concerned with the welfare and future of these students must become familiar with what the research does and does not say about educational practices that are likely to have an impact on important student outcomes (keeping in mind that we take a very broad view of outcomes). There is a great deal of research that we have not discussed in this book—research that describes or analyzes various contexts in which these students live or go to school but that does not make direct and data-based connections to student educational outcomes. If our schools are to substantially improve the academic achievement of ELLs (or any other students for that matter), it is our belief that we must pay closest attention to research that convincingly links what educators do—or can do—to influence important student outcomes. Making this research—which is *not* limited to experimental or statistical research—as accessible as possible to as many people as possible was the primary aim of this book.

Research alone, of course, provides no silver bullet. But it does provide a realistic and necessary foundation for moving forward. It is inevitable that competing beliefs and values, diverging personal experiences, and, yes, prejudices and biases will continue to play roles in the policy and practice debates about English learners and, indeed, about education more generally. Valid and credible research can serve as a ballast to help steady the course. A corollary is that educators and policy makers must ask where the data are when presented with "research-based" practices someone wants them to purchase or adopt. All too often the only response will be a list of publications that might or might not include research and evidence. Even if authors are recognizable, it does not always mean that citations refer to research as opposed to theory or advocacy. It is good to keep in mind the warning "Buyer beware."

Everyone who has an interest in the well-being of these students— parents, community members, leaders, teachers, specialists and coaches, school and district administrators, school board members, and state and federal officials—must be involved and contribute to a comprehensive framework to support their achievement. With this in mind, we offer our final set of recommendations.

# TEACHERS, SPECIALISTS, AND COACHES

- Remember that the foundation of effective practice for ELLs is the same as effective practice *in general*: regardless of language of instruction, ELLs benefit from well-designed, challenging, and structured lessons and activities, with clear purposes, that are relevant, meaningful, and at the appropriate difficulty level, where teachers provide relevant, timely, and useful feedback that improves learning, understanding, and performance. Don't undersell ELLs' academic abilities because they are less than proficient in English.

- At the same time, due primarily to language limitations, ELLs receiving instruction in English will need additional supports to (a) make the academic content accessible and (b) promote their English language development. Build into your lessons the supports discussed in Chapters 3, 4, 5, and 7 and keep lessons at a high and challenging academic level.

- Choose strategies based on an understanding of research-based practices. Well-structured and explicit lessons that cover important academic content are extremely important. Use some amount of materials that are familiar to students, that is, materials dealing with topics they know about from experiences in their homes and communities. Even if you teach in an all-English program, see students' L1 as a resource they can draw on to further their learning. Involve parents and communicate to them how they can support their children's educational success. Some parents, particularly of younger children, can help by providing direct academic support; in other cases they can help by making sure students attend regularly, complete assignments, and put forth needed effort.

- Whether you are teaching in students' L1 or L2, focus on academic language—the language necessary for classroom success—no less than conversational language. Academic language proficiency might be the most significant academic factor in the school success of ELLs.

- Recognize that for many important questions regarding language use in the classroom, research provides little guidance. Thoughtful and systematic experimentation with different instructional strategies, while paying very close attention to impact on student learning, is essential.

- Take advantage of opportunities for professional development, including ongoing mentoring and coaching. Implement new strategies or programs following a recommended sequence and mode of delivery; you might later adapt and modify procedures, but first try to master the strategy and program as it was designed and intended to be used.

- Provide instruction for ELLs throughout the school day. There are three key opportunities for targeted ELL instruction: an ELD time block, sheltered strategies in the content areas, and literacy instruction with texts and other components (e.g., small-group instruction) designed for ELL populations (sometimes referred to as "universal access").

- Administer uniform and consistent assessments of student outcomes in literacy, content areas, and ELD. Although we still face considerable challenges in reliably and validly measuring progress in ELD (Abedi, 2007, 2008) and literacy (August & Shanahan, 2006) for English learners, some sort of progress monitoring is important (e.g., Dutro, 2006). Literacy and ELD for ELLs should be regularly measured, using consistent assessments and benchmarks schoolwide, and used to plan instruction individually by teachers and at grade-level, department, and faculty meetings. Literacy assessments are used for literacy, and ELD assessments to measure proficiency level placement and progress. Reading assessments are not used to measure ELD progress. Confusing these two will mean that ELLs who are fluent readers in L1 and in need of language development may be incorrectly placed with struggling fluent English speakers who need to learn basic literacy skills.

- Work with colleagues at your school to identify important academic goals for ELLs, plan lessons and activities designed to accomplish those goals, then meet to evaluate the lessons' success, using actual student work. Analyze what went well and what did not go well; revise lessons and try again. This can be done in grade-level or department meetings and *needs* to be done throughout the year on a continuous basis.

• Use peer coaching to learn from and help colleagues at school. More generally, participate in a community of learners for making instructional decisions, analyzing assessments, planning, and self-evaluating effective implementation.

• Look for ways to involve the parents of ELLs to support students' school success. Parents want very much for their children to be successful; they are a resource that schools do not typically use fully.

## ADMINISTRATORS AND POLICY MAKERS

• To the extent permitted by state law, encourage academically rigorous primary-language instruction (bilingual education) and the use of the primary language to support academic instruction in English. When state law limits the use of the primary language, work to change it.

• Create schoolwide cultures that emphasize academic achievement for all students, including ELLs. Make learning goals for students tangible, concrete, and focused on important educational outcomes. Specific academic skills are important but so is the integration of skills to demonstrate meaningful learning.

• Support and strongly encourage teachers, specialists, and coaches by making it clear that student achievement—including the achievement of ELLs—is a priority. Do this through regular written and oral communication—formally at meetings and trainings and informally in everyday interactions.

• In order to demonstrate that meaningful student achievement is a priority—not just an occasional rhetorical event—the following must be provided at each school:

   o A regular time and place (including coverage when necessary) for grade-level and department meetings to discuss curriculum and instruction matters for all students and specifically how ELLs will be provided access to core academic content learning

   o Clear expectations that the purpose of these meetings is to focus on academic goals for students, within the framework of district and state standards, and how to help all students progress toward achieving them

   o Necessary on-site assistance or district coaches or consultants who can help teachers move toward accomplishing academic goals with more and more students; outside collaborators such as university researchers for professional development and coaching might be helpful

   o A schoolwide focus and coherence from class to class (such as arranging for cross-class groupings by ELD proficiency levels) or school to school regarding materials, sequencing, and delivery of instruction so that teachers can work on common goals, lessons, and activities

- o Professional development programs and initiatives that are stable (i.e., last for at least three years), well integrated with other school-wide efforts to improve achievement (i.e., are not seen as an additional task to take on), consistent with current research, and provide opportunities for practice and follow-up (includes professional development for district and school administrators in order to support teachers in what they are expected to know and do)
- o Resources and support for parent involvement programs to support the academic program and encourage parents to be active partners in their children's schooling

- Assure that school and district ELL programs follow these guidelines:
  - o Are consistent with current research (or at least are not *inconsistent* with it) in the way we have used research in this book: research that establishes a credible empirical link between educational processes or procedures and student outcomes; remember that qualitative research can establish these links no less than quantitative research
  - o Encourage use of students' home languages, assuming there are qualified personnel, adequate resources, and well-designed programs
  - o Address academic language and not just conversational language
  - o Include daily scheduling of core academic content instruction and dedicated ELD instruction
  - o Use uniform, valid, and instructionally informative accountability measures and benchmarks for student outcomes in literacy, English language development, and other academic areas
  - o Are well supported with personnel, materials, and other resources to support their implementation
  - o Make parents of ELLs feel welcomed and valued at school, with individual schools in particular communicating with home through regular newsletters written in an accessible language

## CONCLUDING THOUGHTS

English learners, their families, communities, and the schools and educators who work with them face significant challenges. Their numbers are increasing, and their achievement lags behind that of many of their peers. But we end on an optimistic note. Over the past decade we have seen a heartening resurgence of research, policy, and professional attention being paid to the educational success of these students. We are hopeful that the polarizing debates over bilingual education can be put behind us and that educators, policy makers, researchers, and the public at large can instead focus on making the best use of the research we have while forging ahead to chart new terrain that will help these students succeed in school and beyond. It is no exaggeration to say that, to a significant degree, the future of our society and economy depends upon it.

## REFERENCES

Abedi, J. (Ed.). (2007). *English language proficiency assessment in the nation: Current status and future practice.* Davis: University of California, Davis.

Abedi, J. (2008). Classification system for English language learners: Issues and recommendations. *Educational Measurement: Issues and Practice, 27*(3), 17–31.

August, D., & Shanahan, T. (Eds.). (2006). *Developing literacy in second-language learners: Report of the National Literacy Panel on language-minority children and youth.* Mahwah, NJ: Lawrence Erlbaum.

Dutro, S. (2006). *ADEPT: A developmental English proficiency test.* San Diego, CA: California Reading and Literature Project.

# Glossary

## Terms Associated With the Education of English Language Learners

**Academic language** is the language associated with school, that is, the language needed to participate in academic instruction and discussions and to be able to read and write texts about academic topics. Academic language is often contrasted with *conversational language*, which tends to be less formal, abstract, and cognitively challenging. The distinction should not be overdrawn, however, since conversational language can also be abstract and cognitively challenging. See **CALP** and **BICS**.

**BICS** (Basic Interpersonal Communicative Skills) is a term coined by Jim Cummins to indicate communication skills used in everyday social interactions, in contrast to the language skills and proficiency required for success in academic contexts. BICS contrasts with **CALP** (see **CALP** entry).

**Bilingual education** includes a number of instructional approaches whereby students who come from non-English-speaking backgrounds receive academic instruction in their **primary**, or home, **language**. In bilingual programs, students are typically taught reading, writing, and other basic skills (e.g., math) in their home language while also receiving English language development (**ELD**; see below) instruction in other academic areas. There are various bilingual education models: transitional bilingual education (students receive primary-language instruction for a period of two to five years and then transition to all-English instruction); maintenance or developmental bilingual education, sometimes called "late exit" (primary-language instruction is maintained throughout elementary school or even beyond); and dual-language or two-way bilingual education, in which students from non-English and English-speaking backgrounds are in the same classes, with the goal of promoting bilingualism, biliteracy, and biculturalism for all students.

**CALP** (Cognitive Academic Language Proficiency) was also coined by Cummins and indicates the type of oral and written language proficiency required for literacy and academic achievement (see **academic language**). CALP contrasts with **BICS** (see previous entry), although the distinction between academic language and conversational language is often not entirely clear-cut (see Table 4.1 in Chapter 4).

**Comprehensible input**, coined by Stephen Krashen, is when a second language being learned is presented in such a way that it is made understandable, despite the person's limitations in the language. In certain instances a second language can naturally become comprehensible because the context makes the meaning relatively clear. However, strategies have been developed to help **ELLs** understand English used during academic instruction, in which the language demands can be considerable. Techniques include context or visual cues, clarification, building background knowledge, and drawing on students' experiences. Comprehensible input is part of **sheltered instruction** (see below).

**Culturally compatible** (or **culturally accommodated**) **instruction** refers to instruction that is intentionally designed to fit, or be compatible with, interactional patterns or learning styles of students from a particular cultural group. For example, if students from a particular group are not used to being expected to answer questions individually in front of a group, culturally compatible instruction would minimize or eliminate situations in which students are called up individually to answer questions in front of the class.

**ELD** (English language development) is instruction designed to promote English language proficiency; formerly known as ESL (English as a second language) instruction.

**ELL** (English language learner) refers to a student from a home where a language other than English is spoken and whose English proficiency is not sufficient to permit the student to be successful in mainstream all-English instruction. Another term used is "limited English proficient," or LEP, but it has fallen into disfavor because of the negative connotations associated with *limited*. "Language minority" is sometimes used to refer to these students, and the term "dual-language learner" is gaining favor.

**English immersion** refers to instruction that is all (or essentially all) in English. English immersion for **ELLs** typically uses **sheltered instruction** to provide **comprehensible input** for content instruction and **ELD** instruction. English immersion is, in principle, very different from English submersion (or "sink or swim"), in which students are provided no or little support and are basically on their own to learn academic content during classroom instruction. In the 1974 decision *Lau v. Nichols*, the Supreme Court effectively determined that "sink or swim" violates student rights under the 1964 Civil Rights Act and is therefore illegal.

**Primary language** is a student's home language, typically the first ("primary") language a student has been exposed to and learned to understand and speak. The primary language is sometimes referred to as L1, in contrast to a second language, which is referred to as L2.

**Primary-language instruction** refers to providing academic instruction in a student's **primary language**. **Bilingual education** in the United States comprises primary-language instruction and instruction in English.

**Primary-language support** occurs when students are in essentially all-English instruction, but the teacher uses students' primary language to assist learning content in English. Primary-language support can include a number of different strategies and techniques, for example, using words that are cognates in English and the student's **primary language** (e.g., *democracy* and *democracia*), previewing a lesson in the primary language followed by teaching the lesson in English, and teaching comprehension or learning strategies in the primary language followed by students applying them in English.

**Sheltered instruction** comprises a set of strategies and techniques used to help **ELLs** learn academic content that is taught in English, despite students' being less than fully English proficient. These strategies can include the use of graphic organizers, redundant visual cues, explicit classroom organizational strategies, language and content objectives, and primary-language support. The goal of sheltered instruction is to make grade-level content (that is, *not* simple or watered-down content) comprehensible to ELLs. An important, but secondary goal is to help promote English language proficiency as students learn academic content. In California, sheltered instruction is known as SDAIE, or Specially Designed Academic Instruction in English.

**Sociocultural** influences refer to the wide range of (nonbiological) factors that determine the social contexts in which children and youth live and go to school. These contexts are defined, or influenced, by such things as a sociocultural group's beliefs, attitudes, behaviors, and practices, which are often related to social and political circumstances, material (or economic) resources, and ethnic, cultural, or national origin and identity. Any of these factors, and in virtually any combination, can constitute sociocultural influences and define a particular sociocultural group.

**Transfer** is a concept from cognitive and educational psychology referring to the process whereby what you learn in one context or setting influences what you know, are able to do, or the ease with which you can learn in another context or setting. There is positive transfer, for example, in the fact that learning to read in your **primary language** helps you learn to read in a second language, since so many skills transfer across languages. But there is also negative transfer: Although Spanish and English use essentially the same alphabet and many of the sounds represented by letters are identical or similar (thereby promoting positive transfer), some letters represent different sounds in the two languages or have no corresponding sounds in one or the other language (e.g., vowels have only one sound each in Spanish but can represent different sounds in English, depending on the word).

# *Index*

**CORWIN**

A SAGE Company

The Corwin logo—a raven striding across an open book—represents the union of courage and learning. Corwin is committed to improving education for all learners by publishing books and other professional development resources for those serving the field of PreK–12 education. By providing practical, hands-on materials, Corwin continues to carry out the promise of its motto: **"Helping Educators Do Their Work Better."**